Περι ενεργειασ δαιμονων διαλογος

De Operatione Dæmonum

dialogues de energia seu operatione dæmonum

The Source Works of Ceremonial Magic series:

Volume   I - The Practical Angel Magic of John Dee's Enochian
           Tables - ISBN 978-0-9547639-0-9

Volume II – The Keys to the Gateway of Magic: Summoning the Solomonic
           Archangels & Demonic Princes – ISBN 978-0-9547639-1-6

Volume III – The Goetia of Dr Rudd: The Angels & Demons of *Liber
           Malorum Spirituum seu Goetia* – ISBN 978-0-9547639-2-3

Volume IV – The Veritable Key of Solomon– ISBN 978-0-9547639-8-5
           (leather) also available as 978-0-7378-1453-0 (cloth)

Volume V – The Grimoire of Saint Cyprian - ISBN 978-0-9557387-1-5
           (cloth) ISBN 978-0-9557387-4-6 (limited leather edition)

Volume VI – Sepher Raziel: Liber Salomonis (English grimoire 1564)
           – ISBN 978-0-9557387-3-9 (cloth) – ISBN 978-0-9557387-5-3
           (leather)

For further details of forthcoming volumes in this series, edited
from classic magical manuscripts see www.GoldenHoard.com

"It is said that nature or natural reason, persuades the sacred dæmons, and in a word, all that proceeds from the God who is good in Himself, to be beneficent."

- George Gemistos Plethon in his *Commentary on the Chaldaean Oracles*

Michael Psellus

Dialogue on the Operation of Dæmons

Translated from the original Greek by
Marcus Collisson

Edited by
Stephen Skinner

GOLDEN HOARD PRESS
2010

Published by Golden Hoard Press
PO Box 1073
Robinson Road PO
Singapore 902123

www.GoldenHoard.com

First written in Greek circa 1050

First Greek & Latin Edition 1615

First Published in English 1843

Second Edition in English 2010

ISBN: 978-0-9557387-2-2

Printed in Malaysia

Acknowledgements

I wish to acknowledge the helpfulness of the staff of the Nicholson Museum of Antiquities at Sydney University, and the detailed and painstaking subediting of this text by Zoe Low of Johor Bahru. My thanks to Jim Baker for first pointing out the value of this text.

Contents

Introduction

Why are we publishing this long neglected and rather obscure work? The reason is neatly summed up by John Duffy:[1]

> "The extraordinary thing about Psellos is that, single-handedly, he was responsible for bringing back, almost from the dead, an entire group of occult authors and books whose existence had long been as good as forgotten. Between the time of Photios[2] in the ninth and the arrival of Psellos in the eleventh century, one would be hard put to find in extant Byzantine sources any references to Hermes Trismegistus and the *Hermetica*,[3] to Julius Africanus and the *Kestoi*,[4] to Proclus' *De Arte Hieratica*,[5] or to the *Chaldaean Oracles*,[6] that is, the authors and works that were the classics in the field of mysticism and magic."

Or to put it more simply, Psellus was the bridge between Neo-Platonic, Gnostic and Hermetic texts and the theology, philosophy and dæmonology of the late Byzantine era: a bridge between the classical view of the dæmon as a beneficial guiding spiritual presence, and the later Christian view of demons as intrinsically evil fallen angels. Byzantine magic was later destined to be the source of the main grimoires of Western European magic from the 14th century onwards.

---

[1] In John Duffy, 'Reactions of Two Byzantine intellectuals to the Theory and Practice of Magic: Michael Psellos and Michael Italikos' in *Byzantine Magic* edited by Henry Maguire, Dumbarton Oaks, Washington, 1995.

[2] Photios the Great, Patriarch of Constantinople c. 810 – c. 893.

[3] *Hermetica* are a series of primarily Greek Gnostic and wisdom literature dating from around the second and third centuries of the Christian era which are often attributed to Hermes Trismegistus, Hermes, Tat, or Asclepius. These were compiled into a *Corpus Hermeticum* during the Renaissance, notably by Marsilio Ficino.

[4] An encyclopaedic work supposedly by Julius Africanus on practical subjects like agriculture, natural history, military science, tactics, medicine and veterinary.

[5] On the magical practices ascribed to the Chaldaeans.

[6] A fragmentary selection of sayings which have been attributed to Zoroaster, but are probably of more recent compilation. Before the 17th century these basically pagan and theurgically orientated passages were considered of great antiquity, and part of an older theology, and even accepted by he Church.

Up until the arrival of the Arabs in the 7th century, the Byzantine empire was regarded as one of the strongest economies of Europe, particularly known for being the primary western terminus of the famous silk road from China. Its intellectual legacies derived from classical Greek philosophy and mythology, Orthodox Christianity, and the long Greek occupation of Egypt, which brought with it a mix of Graeco-Egyptian magic. These influences later helped lay the foundations for the Italian Renaissance, and also of the grimoire tradition.

Psellus was a man of great intelligence, serving as a political advisor to a succession of Byzantine Emperors. He became the leading professor at the newly founded University of Constantinople, bearing the honorary title, 'Consul of the Philosophers', and was the driving force behind the university curriculum reform designed to emphasize the Greek classics, especially Homeric and Neo-Platonic literature, rather than Christian theology and apologetics. Psellus was adept in politics, astronomy, medicine, music, theology, jurisprudence, physics, grammar, magic and dæmonology.

We are lucky that Michael Psellus (1018-1096 C.E.) not only wrote histories of his own time, but also included a large amount of autobiographical material as well. He was born in Constantinople to an aristocratic family which included members of the consular and patrician elite. He was given the name Constantine, a family name which also recalled the Emperor Constantine, who made Christianity the state religion of Rome. It is interesting that when he entered the Bithynia monastery, he chose Michael, the name of the Archangel responsible for controlling demons, as his monastic name. He received a classical, as well as Christian, education in Constantinople and Athens. His teacher, John Mauropus, was well connected and enabled the young Psellus to meet with students who later became Patriarchs (Constantine Leichoudes and John Xiphilinos), and even Emperors (Constantine X Doukas).

For a while he served in the provinces as a judge, but his career was to be primarily at the Imperial Court, punctuated by short spells in a monastery, when he was temporarily out of favour. Before 1042 he returned to Constantinople, where he became a secretary in the imperial chancellery. He rose from this position rapidly to become an influential political advisor to Emperor Constantine IX Monomachos (reigned 1042-1055). Towards the end of Monomachos' reign, Psellus decided for political reasons to leave the court, entering the Olympus monastery in Bithynia in 1054. Upon Monomachos' death he was soon recalled to court by his successor, Empress Theodora (reigned 1055-1056).

Psellus is extraordinary in as much as he was able to serve successive Emperors and Empresses as a high-ranking political advisor without apparently losing his political influence when they changed. It is often said that to achieve this he must have been a servile flatterer, but it is more likely that he achieved this through the quickness of his apprehension of the priorities of the reigning monarch, whoever that might be.

He smoothed the way, playing a decisive political role in the transition of power from Michael VI to Isaac I Komnenos in 1057; then from Isaac Komnenos to his old friend Constantine X Doukas (1059); and then again from Romanos IV Diogenes to Michael VII Doukas (1071). Psellus continued to serve a succession of Emperors till the mid-1070s when his political power waned, and his autobiographical narrative ceased. Many scholars think that this absence of information means that Psellus died soon after the fall of Michael VII in 1078, although other scholars have proposed later dates such as 1096.

Psellus' literary output was prodigious. Many of his works remain in manuscript and have not been printed. They can be categorised as follows:[1]

1. Histories. Many feel that his most important works were his histories of the Byzantine rulers, many of whom he knew personally and served. The best known of these books is his *Chronographia*,[2] a history of the fourteen Byzantine emperors and empresses, during the century preceding Psellus' own time, from the reign of Basil II,

[1] A complete list of his works is given in Fabricius, *Bibliotheca Graeca*, x.41.
[2] *Chronographia* translated by E.R.A. Sewter, Penguin, London, 1982.

the "Bulgar-Slayer" (976-1025) till the 1070s. This work also includes extensive autobiographical material.

Historia Syntomos was another shorter historical text from his pen in the form of a world chronicle.

2. A large number of scientific treatises on astronomy, anatomy, medicine (one notable medical essay listed hundreds of symptoms and illnesses), music, psychology, geography (a topography of Athens) and physics.

3. Philosophical and religious treatises. Of these, the present text, *De Operatione Dæmonum*, is probably the best known. His commentary on Aristotle's Philosophy, *Peri Hermeneias* was also well known. His studies of laography, of old customs, particularly folkloric and religious also fit here.

4. Texts on jurisprudence, stemming from his time as a provincial judge, including a poetic compendium of law and an explanation of legal terms.

5. Funeral orations (*epitaphioi*) over the patriarchs Michael Keroularios, Constantine III Leichoudes, John Xiphilinos, and his own mother.

6. Speeches and panegyrics often addressed to the ruling Emperor or his current court patron. These included works against the Bogomils and Euchites. His fascination with these heresies also surfaces in the present work.

7. Satirical and epigrammatic verse and essays, including didactic poems on formal topics such as grammar, Greek dialects and rhetoric.

8. A fragmentary encyclopaedia, called 'Manifold Teaching' (*Didaskalia Pantodape*).

9. Literary works like a paraphrase of Homer's *Iliad*.

10. About five hundreds personal letters.

He was truly a Renaissance man equally at home with the intrigues of the court, or the subtleties of philosophy and religion (both pagan Greek and Christian).

Paganism and Christianity

Although on the face of it an Orthodox Christian, Psellus had a high regard for the pagan gods and the Platonic and neo-Platonic philosophers. His interest in Plato and Aristotle lead him to the neo-Platonists Plotinus, Porphyry, Iamblichus and Proclus. Finally Psellus explored the *Chaldaean Oracles* (a text from circa the second century C.E. attributed to the two Julians), with its mixture of philosophy, cosmology, hierarchy of gods and spirits, and theurgy or divine magic. Duffy outlines Psellus' interest in theurgy in a description which is replete with the techniques of magic:

> "In another type of ritual, again according to information supplied by Psellos, the theurgist used statues of specific deities in order to establish contact with them. The process of making contact involved, among other things, special stones, herbs, animals, and sometimes aromatic substances (*aromata*), which were places inside the effigy. Stones and herbs were also used in other rituals to scare away bad demons or to purify the soul. Iamblichus tells us that in the art of theurgy certain materials – specific stones, plants, animals, and aromatic substances (*aromata*) – were regarded as especially suitable for attracting the presence of divinities."[1]

Psellus comments, in a feeble effort to justify his interest, that the *Oracles* are "correct and full of Christian teaching". That comment is typical of his thinking which attempted to blend the ancient philosophers with more recent Christian doctrines, although he characterised them as "these ideas I have taken from the *Chaldaean Oracles* and have subordinated to our Christian scriptures."[2] He seems to have had a greater interest in the former rather than the later, and at one point Psellus was almost excommunicated for his over zealous interest in astrology, pagan philosophy and theurgy. While admitting that he knew astrology (frowned upon by the Church) and the correct theurgic rituals to infuse life in a statue, he declined to give details, explaining that his readers might get into

---

[1] Duffy, John, 'Reactions of Two Byzantine Intellectuals to the Theory and Practice of Magic: Michael Psellos and Michael Italikos' in *Byzantine Magic* edited by Henry Maguire, Dumbarton Oaks, Washington, 1995, page 85.
[2] K. N. Sathas, *Mesaionike Bibliotheke*, V, 449 as quoted by Duffy.

trouble if they used it. He does however hint at the part perfumes play in the process:

> "From my reading of Hellenic literature I know that perfumes (*aromata*) give off a vapour which drives away evil spirits and which at the same time restores to the materials affected by it the presence of more benign spirits. In the same way, in other cases, stones and herbs and mystic rites induce apparitions of divinities."[1]

Such procedures designed to conjure apparitions of divinities come directly out of second century Graeco-Egyptian magical texts. Rituals used to vivify the statues of angels (particularly the angel Michael who was worshipped as a god in his own right in Asia Minor) are similar. At a practical level it was sometimes difficult to distinguish the two.

Magic and Miracles

Magic and miracles share the same techniques even if not always the same sponsorship. It is not sufficient to distinguish them one from the other by saying one appeals to the aid of angels (or God) while the other appeals to the aid of dæmons: both utilise the help of 'spiritual creatures' to achieve something outside the realm of the accepted norm. [2]

How then is one to distinguish between magic and miracles? This is a problem that has bedevilled the Church from the earliest of times. Even during the life of Jesus there were often disputes, as to the nature of his miracles, and to their source. One group of Pharisees were of the opinion that Jesus utilised Beelzebub to perform his miracles.[3] In fact it is not sufficient to say that miracles are done by saints and magic by magicians, or even to claim that miracles have always have beneficial results and magic not always so.

---

[1] Psellus, *Chronographia*, Book VI, chapters 65-67 as quoted by Duffy.

[2] The term 'spiritual creatures' is used in the sense Dr John Dee understood it: the whole spectrum of non-physical creatures from imps, elementals, spirits, angels, and dæmons. –Ed.

[3] *Matthew* 12:24-27 records this event. Interestingly, Jesus did not deny that he used a dæmon, but simply asked the Pharisees which dæmon they or their children used. –Ed.

What can be said with certainty is that in the early days of Christianity, or the last days of paganism (whichever way you wish to look at it) there was a lot of competition between practitioners on both sides of the fence, and much of this took place in the Eastern Christian Empire, or Greek Byzantium.

Let us look at the actions of just two of St Paul's most active Greek disciples, Jason and Sosipatros. Jason was from Tarsus (in Asia Minor or modern day Turkey) as was St Paul. Sosipatros was a native of Patra, Achaia, part of northern Arcadia in Greece. He is thought to be the same Sosipater who is mentioned in *Acts* 20:4. They both became disciples of St Paul, who even went so far as to call them his kinsmen (*Romans* 16:21), and so their approach was probably very close to the official Christian line on miracles and magic.

> "There is a little-known '*vita* and martyrdom' of two of St. Paul's disciples, Jason and Sosipatros, the central episode of which represents a contest between a pagan magician and the Christian martyrs.[1] Unlike the legend about Pope Sylvester, in Jason and Sosipatros' *vita* it is the pagan sorcerer who works a humane and creative miracle, plowing and sowing a field that within an hour produced a crop; from this grain the sorcerer immediately baked some bread. By contrast, the Christian miracle was cruel and destructive: the saints burned a palace with its inhabitants and murdered the magician. Certainly, in this case the destruction and death could [apparently] be justified since the victims were heathen... Be that as it may, the pagan magician was here a provider of food, and the disciples of St. Paul arsonists and killers."[2]

It is clear therefore that the distinction between magic and miracles cannot be made on the basis of results. Let us look at some of the 'spiritual creatures' involved.

---

[1] *Bibliotheca Hagiographica Graeca* 776, published in Doukakes, *Megas Synaxariastes*, Athens, April 1892, pages 438-456.
[2] Alexander Kazhdan, 'Holy and Unholy Miracle Workers' in *Byzantine Magic* edited by Henry Maguire, Dumbarton Oaks, Washington, 1995, page 79.

Dæmons

Dæmons are amongst the spiritual creatures that are involved in works of magic, and possibly also in the production of miracles. In this work Psellus introduces a classification system of dæmons. According to Psellus, this division dates back to Plato and before. There are six different types of dæmons:

1. igneous (fiery).
2. aerial (airy).
3. terrestrial (earthy).
4. aqueous (watery).
5. subterranean (underground).
6. heliophobic (those adverse to sunlight).

In this categorisation you can see the four classical elements, Fire, Air, Earth and Water, plus a further two categories of dæmons who 'flee the light'. [1] This is much simpler than the Hebraic Kabbalistic or grimoire division of dæmons.[2] The classical Greek view however is that the dæmons occupy the space between the heavens and earth, and are therefore sub-lunary, or 'under the Moon'.

The Platonic view was that each person had a personal dæmon, who acted to help and preserve that person. With the rise of Orthodox Christianity, the concept of a personal dæmon transformed itself into the idea of the Holy Guardian Angel, a concept which re-appears in the practices of the 19th century Golden Dawn.

A more wide ranging view is that they acted as messengers between man and the gods. Plato explains the special powers belonging to dæmons:

> "They [the dæmons] act, as interpreters and conveyers of human things to the gods, of divine things to men. They carry the prayers and sacrifices of men, the commandments of the gods and their responses to the sacrifices: Occupying a place between the two, they

---

[1] Often referred to as *lucifugous*.
[2] For which see Stephen Skinner, *The Complete Magicians Tables*, Golden Hoard Press, Singapore, 2006, Tables K and M.

fill up a gap and cause the whole universe to be a coherent whole. All divination takes place by their means, the art of priests, the art of sacrifices and mystical rites and incantations; in a word, all divining and magic. A god has no immediate relation with a man, all converse between men and gods, whether in a waking state or in sleep, takes place through the Dæmon-kind."[1]

In doing so Plato characterizes dæmons as messengers. But that is exactly what angels are, messengers between man and god. Here we again see that angels and dæmons are part of a continuum of 'spiritual creatures'. Their importance in magic and divination is also here mentioned by Plato.

In the *Epinomis*, Plato further explains their messenger status in terms of interpretation of the words of men to the gods and vice versa:

> "The dæmon-kind occupies the intermediate region between men and gods, and is the agent of interpretation: it [the dæmon] is therefore to be specially honoured by prayer in order that the right words [of prayer or invocation] may get through...the whole sky [sub-lunary world] is full of living beings, they act as interpreters of everything to each other and to the supreme gods."[2]

Angels

The Bible is replete with references to angels. As Glen Peers puts it:

> Scripture is unequivocal in stating the existence of an angelic host and is full of diverse examples of the appearance of these transcendental creatures.[3]

Like djinn they were often said to be composed of fire and air. Of the angels mentioned in the *Old Testament,* only three were named: Michael, Raphael and Gabriel. Of these the most important was Michael, who is elsewhere characterised as a subduer of demons, or of 'fallen' angels. Michael was venerated in Egypt, but was also the

---

[1] The seeress Diotima of Mantanea's discussion in Plato, *Symposium*, 202E.
[2] Plato, *Epinomis*, 984E-985B. This text is attributed to Plato, but may be by Philip of Opus.
[3] Glen Peers, *Subtle Bodies*, University of California Press, Berkeley, 2001, page 1.

most popular angel in the Byzantine world, and an object of devotion in a cult of the Archangel Michael which rose to prominence at Colossae (later Chonae) in Turkey. The early Christian church struggled with a cult of the angels which they feared may have allowed pagan worshippers to equate their old gods with specific angels. St. Paul's *Epistle to the Colossians* was specifically directed against this type of angelolatry. Michael Psellus however wrote a work specifically praising his namesake Archangel, and claiming to feel his presence near to his shrine at Colossae or Galatia in Turkey. [1] The worship of angels was sometimes considered acceptable, sometimes heretical.

The Church's attitude to dæmons was that they only had power granted by god to trick people into following them, whereas the popular, and indeed magical view, was that dæmons had the power to do things in their own right. The generally accepted Byzantine ecclesiastical opinion of the day was that dæmons were angels who had fallen or been banished from heaven, rather than Plato's much older view of dæmons as guardians or messengers between man and the gods. Once you have posited 'war in heaven', with a number of angels rebelling, and the angel Michael routing and banishing the rebellious angels, then you have created the possibility of a dualist theology. The most pervasive dualist theology that was current in Byzantium at that time was Bogomilism.

The Bogomils

The Slavic word 'bogomil' simply means 'dear to god', although some have suggested the existence a founder of the heresy with that name. Bogomilism arose in the mid tenth century in Macedonia, which was then under Bulgarian authority. Because of their violent rule, indignation and dissatisfaction were inevitable and this made it a popular movement which had an anti-church and anti-feudal bias. Its members repudiated church and state control and desired to live a simple modest life, rejecting the Old Testament and the works of

---

[1] Psellus, *Oratio in Archangelum Michaelem* in *Michaelis Pselli 'Orationes Hagiographicae'*, edited E. A. Fisher, Stuttgart & Leipzig, 1994, pages 230-256.

the Church Fathers, the saints, the cult of the Virgin Mary, and most prayers. Because of persecution, a number of Bogomils fled to Byzantium. Bogomilism spread first throughout Bulgaria and Bosnia, then to Italy and finally to southern France, where Catharism was to influence the course of history.

For the origin of this heresy and the reason for its strength in Macedonia and Thrace we have to look back three centuries. In the seventh century a Gnostic sect, incorporating elements of Mani's dualist teachings, named the Pavlikianis, was active in Armenia. This sect was seen as a threat to the state and so the Tsars Constantine V Kopronim (741-775) and Ivan Cimiskes (969-976) forcibly removed them to Thrace and Macedonia, thus creating the two centres of dualist heresies remarked upon by Psellus.

Psellus seems to have been fascinated by the dualist heresies of the Euchitæ and the Bogomils. For someone with a strong interest in both angels and dæmons, the dualist roots of these heresies must have been a matter of considerable interest. The basic dualist premise is that there is a good god and a bad god. This approach solves the questions of 'how was evil allowed to come into being' and 'how were the angels allowed to rebel in the first place', if there is only one all-powerful god, a question not easily answered by orthodox religion.

There is of course another explanation for the creation of dæmons, the old Hebraic tradition, to be found in *Genesis 6, I Enoch* and *Jubilees*, which tells the story of the angels descending to Earth to mate with the daughters of men, whose offspring were giants. This is followed up in the confessions of some of the dæmons which appear in the *Testament of Solomon.*

Bogomil mythology stated that Satanael was the first-born son of God the Father, who before rebelling sat enthroned upon his right hand. The original Greek for this first-born son is Σαταναηλ Satanael, not Σατανασ Satan, and so the translator has done a disservice to Psellus by simply translating this word as Satan. The place of Satanael as master of this world is confirmed by the passage in the Bible where he offers Christ all the kingdoms of this Earth, an offer he could not credibly make if they were not his to offer.[1] Satanael eventually tried to assume too much power and was ejected from heaven.[2]

After the Fall, Satanael created the world, with all its plants and animals. He formed Adam from mud, but failed to animate him. He appealed to god the Father who animated Adam with the divine spirit. This neatly explains how the body can be from one god but the spirit from another. As their bodies were evil by nature, according to this doctrine, few men ever reached heaven.

The Euchitæ on the other hand have three gods, the Father and two sons, one with power over heaven and the other with power over the Earth and material things.

Pseudo-Psellus

A number of scholars, like Bidez and Gautier, are of the opinion that Michael Psellus was not the author of the present work, but another writer of the late thirteenth or early fourteenth century (specifically the Palaeologan period). Accordingly the author of this work is sometimes referred to as 'Pseudo-Psellus'. I prefer to reserve judgement on that issue till proof is forthcoming, or at least a concrete suggestion of another candidate for authorship is made. It is often the case that unknown authors will affix the names of more illustrious writers to their works in order to sell more copies. On the other hand, it is also the case that critics will dismiss a work as not being by a particular author simply because it does not seem 'appropriate' or in keeping with their private image of that author.

There is also some confusion with a non-existent Michael Psellus the Elder, the product of an unfounded academic supposition.

It is worth mentioning that Psellus's name in Greek Ψελλός also leads to his name being transliterated as 'Psellos' which is perhaps a more correct transliteration, but here we will stick to the more familiar and widespread Latinised 'Psellus'.

---

[1] Luke 4:5.
[2] Some Bogomils identified the characteristics of Satanael with the god of the Old Testament.

Psellus's Legacy

Psellus was important in his promotion of Platonic and neo-Platonic ideas, and to the transmission of the *Corpus Hermeticum*. In fact scholars like Reitzenstein think that most of the 14th century Greek manuscripts of that text were derived from the copy owned by Psellus.

Psellus also influenced Francesco Maria Guazzo, an Italian priest from Milan who wrote the infamous *Compendium Maleficarum*,[1] a volume that was to have an enduring influence upon witch-finders and magistrates for centuries to come. Guazzo used Psellus as a source of information on the classification of demons. But Guazzo's text went much further than Psellus' measured description of demons, and became a textbook for the 17th century witch persecutions. Many of the descriptions of the activities of witches (much of it imaginary) in that book have found their way into modern witchcraft literature, and into the fiction of modern writers like Dennis Wheatley.

Samuel Taylor Coleridge's took note of Psellus in his epic poem *The Rime of the Ancient Mariner*, where he refers to him as "the Platonic Constantinopolitan, Michael Psellus" who he credits as an authority on "the invisible inhabitants of this planet, neither departed souls nor angels", thereby coyly avoiding the use of the word 'demon'.

The Translator

Marcus Collisson flourished circa 1841-1876, and lived in various parts of New Zealand and the Australian colonies (as they were then) including, Queensland, South Australia and New South Wales. He was described as a writer, lecturer and publisher, and may have even tried his hand at preaching. It is rather perplexing that his name is spelled in two different ways. Even in the first edition of the present publication, he is spelled 'Collisson' in two places, but as 'Collison'

---

[1] *Compendium Maleficarum, Ex quo nefandissima in genus humanum opera venefica, ac ad illa vitanda remedia conspiciuntur.* Per Fratrem Franciscum Mariam Guaccium Ord. S. Ambrosij ad Nemus Mediolani compilatum, 1626. Reprinted London, 1929, edited by Montague Summers.

on the front title label. One has to assume that the double 's' is correct as it is more likely that he proofed the interior of the book, but did not see the cover label till it was too late, given the mechanics of the book publishing process.

Collisson appears to have moved from Sydney to South Australia soon after publishing the Psellus translation, where he published two books in 1844-46: *A Description of the actual state of the Colony, of its sources of wealth, etc* and *The Miner's Manual*, dedicated to His Excellency George Grey, Lieutenant Governor of New Zealand.

This indicates rather a wide range of publishing interests, and patrons. Collisson is referred to in contemporary documents as an editor and publisher rather than as a translator. Maybe the ambiguous spacing of the dedication to the classicist Dr Nicholson on the title page suggests that the latter had more of a hand in the translation than Collisson indicates.

Collisson had originally been expected to become a vicar in the Church of England, and would have learned Greek for that purpose. It may have been that Collisson even flirted with Baptist belief, as a snippet in a recent Australian publication suggests:

> "David McLaren left the colony in 1841 and the congregation split over the 'close communion' issue. W. Finlayson, in whose home the Baptist meetings were first held, along with a group of others, went elsewhere. Angas sent Marcus Collis[s]on to take over from McLaren in the church, but he proved quite unsatisfactory."[1]

South Australia's first purely religious newspaper appeared in 1845. It was simply called *Australiana*, apparently founded by a shadowy clergyman named Milne, and printed by the prolific George Dehane. It was later taken over by Marcus Collisson, and much of the content of those issues consists of tirades against Roman Catholicism. It is therefore ironic that later in his life, in 1876, a newsletter records

---

[1] 'Scotch Baptists, Church of Christ and Disciples' in *The Australian Christian*, 4 November, 1995.

Marcus Collisson's conversion to Catholicism: [1]

> "From Queensland we hear of the conversion of Mr. Marcus Collison [*sic*], the well-known writer and lecturer. Mr. Collison is a graduate of Trinity College, Dublin, and at one time it was intended that he should become a minister of the Church of England. He was educated with strong anti-Catholic prejudices, and amongst his earlier works may be mentioned a pamphlet on "Papal Aggression."

The present translation was, in a rather strange way, dedicated by Marcus Collisson to Dr Charles Nicholson. With this dedication arises the suspicion that Nicholson might have had more of a hand in the translation that was stated by Collisson, especially as Nicholson had a much more prominent reputation as a classical Greek scholar than Collisson, and Byzantine Greek is not the simplest of languages.

Charles Nicholson

Sir Charles Nicholson (1808-1903) was a statesman, landowner, businessman, collector, linguist, scholar and physician. He was an only son and born in Cockermouth, Cumberland, England. The families of both his mother and father were merchants. Both parents died when he was very young, and he was brought up by a maiden aunt in Yorkshire. He studied medicine at the University of Edinburgh, and passed with flying colours, coming in second, and graduating in 1833.

Later that year he sailed for Sydney to live with his maternal uncle, Captain James Ascough, who was an extensive land owner on the Hawkesbury and Hunter Rivers in New South Wales. Having inherited most of his uncle's property on his death, he devoted his attention to buying land and stock and establishing sheep stations. He also helped establish shipping and railway companies.

In 1836 he was among the founders of the Australian Gaslight Company, and became a trustee of the Australian Museum. Seven years later in 1843 he was elected a member of the Legislative Council, and was elected Speaker in 1846. Nicholson was therefore

---

[1] *New Zealand Tablet*, Rōrahi III, Putanga 142, 21 Kohitātea, 1876, Page 10. Despite the spelling of the surname there is little doubt that it is the same person.

the unusual combination of 'man of affairs' and scholar, as he was deeply interested in the classics, history and education.

Nicholson's name is indissolubly connected with the founding of my *alma mater* the University of Sydney. "It was said that Douglass moved Wentworth, Wentworth moved the Legislative Council, and Nicholson moved heaven and earth; and between them, finally, on the 1st October, 1850, success was achieved, the Royal Assent was given to the Act of Incorporation" of Sydney University. Nicholson was appointed Vice-Provost of the University from 1851 to 1854 and Provost (later Chancellor) from 1854 to 1862. He further benefited the University through his gift of the Nicholson Museum of Antiquities to the University in 1857. This museum focuses to a large extent on Greek and Egyptian antiquities, which were his passion.

Later he acted for some forty years as the university's agent in England, selecting staff and adding periodically to the library and to the Museum of Antiquities. In the same year, back in England, he secured for the University of Sydney a Royal Charter (1857) giving its degrees equal status with those of the old British universities of Oxford and Cambridge.

His interest in Egyptology is reflected in the Museum and artifacts he presented to the University. In 1855-58 he was in Egypt, where he visited many archaeological sites. He was closely involved with the Egyptologists Sayce and Petrie and supported the Egyptian Exploration Fund. In the early 1880s he took up the study of Hebrew, to add to his knowledge of Greek and Latin, and in 1891 he published a handsome volume entitled *Ægyptiaca, Comprising a Catalogue of Egyptian Antiquities ... now Deposited in the Museum of Sydney.*

He became a leading member of the Royal Colonial Institute, the Royal Society of Arts, the British Association, and many other learned and cultural bodies. He was knighted in 1852, created a baronet in 1859, and held honorary degrees from the Universities of Oxford, Cambridge and Edinburgh.

Editing Conventions

Footnotes by the translator have been rendered exactly as they were except that footnotes are numbered rather than being indicated by asterisks or dagger symbols. Footnotes introduced by the present editor are indicated by the addition of '-Ed.' Square brackets were introduced by the translator to indicate words not in the original Greek, but thought necessary for a full understanding of the text. The present editor has introduced more such expansions in square brackets, as less knowledge of such subjects can now be taken for granted, as the standards of Classical education are much lower than they were in the nineteenth century. There is no distinction made between such expansions by the editor or by the translator. Book titles have been systematically italicised for clarity, rather than being enclosed in quote marks or simply left in plain Roman font, as they were in the original text. Some paragraph breaks have been silently introduced to facilitate ease of reading.

The typography of the original title page has been adhered to as closely as possible, to give the flavour of book production at the time when the translation was first published. Otherwise the text has been rendered in Book Antigua with Times Roman footnotes throughout.

The Archangel St. Michael's fight against the Dragon by Albrecht Dürer.
This Archangel has always been credited with the power to control demons.

PSELLUS' DIALOGUE

ON THE

OPERATION OF DÆMONS;

NOW, FOR THE FIRST TIME,

TRANSLATED INTO ENGLISH

FROM THE ORIGINAL GREEK,

AND

ILLUSTRATED WITH NOTES,

BY

MARCUS COLLISSON.

SYDNEY:

PUBLISHED BY JAMES TEGG, BOOKSELLER AND STATIONER,

AND

PRINTED BY D. L. WELCH,
AT THE ATLAS-OFFICE, OPPOSITE THE POST-OFFICE,

Of whom the work may be had.

MDCCCXLIII.

The Translator is willing to devote a few hours daily to private tuition. — His course of instruction would include, besides the Classics, a general English Education. Communications addressed to MARCUS COLLISSON, may be left at either Mr. Tegg's, Bookseller, Mr. Welch, Printer, opposite the Post-office, or Mr. Sands, Print-seller, George-street, [Sydney].

Subscribers are informed, that owing to the work being enlarged by additional matter in the Introduction and Notes, the price will be Two Shillings.

[Original advertisement in the 1843 first edition]

Sydney, February, 1843.

SIR,

Your kindness to a stranger at this extremity of the globe, and your well-known encouragement of general literature, induce me to dedicate this Translation of Psellus' *Dialogue on Dæmons*, as a small, but sincere token of grateful acknowledgment, hoping you will extend that indulgence which first literary attempts seem to call for.

I have the honour to be,

Sir,

Your obliged and obedient humble Servant,

THE TRANSLATOR.

DR. CHARLES NICHOLSON.

INTRODUCTORY PREFACE

MICHÆL PSELLUS, who flourished in the eleventh century, the Author of this little treatise on the operation of Dæmons, was an eminent philologist, philosopher, and scholar, and filled the office of Tutor to the young Prince Michael, son of Constantine Ducas,[1] with great credit to himself, as appears from the eulogium passed on him by Anna Comnena,[2] daughter of the emperor Alexis (*Alexiados*, lib. v.) Beside other works, he wrote an exposition of Aristotle's *Philosophy*, and Commentaries on the *Book of Psalms* and Solomon's *Song*. Mosheim, the ecclesiastical historian, pays the following tribute to his worth: —

"But the greatest ornament of the Republic of Letters in the eleventh century was Michael Psellus, a man illustrious in every respect, and deeply versed in all the various kinds of erudition that were known in his age. This great man recommended warmly to his countrymen the study of philosophy, and particularly the system of Aristotle, which he embellished and illustrated in several learned and ingenious productions."

The work (now for the first time published in an English dress) was written A. D. about 1050, and was distinguished by the learned Barthius with the honourable title, 'The Little Golden Book.' It is interesting as a literary curiosity, being now exceedingly scarce, as well as by its subject, on which mankind have generally shown themselves very inquisitive. It is further interesting from its detailing most minutely the extraordinary secret proceedings of the Euchitæ,

---

[1] Byzantine co-Emperor (c.1074 – c.1090 C.E.) - Ed.
[2] Anna Komnene (1083–1153 C.E.) was a scholar and historian.

otherwise called Massalians [1] (which, it must be admitted, is a *desideratum*), and it seems to determine the true meaning of the expression "doctrines of dæmons" (*1st Tim[othy]. iv., 1*).

We may further remark respecting the work, it may be considered a fair specimen of the manner in which heathen philosophy was blended with Christian theology in the author's day, and of the plausible reasonings with which the most absurd theories were supported; and it goes far to show that certain terms, which by ecclesiastical usage have obtained a harsh signification, had not acquired such harsh signification so early as the period for which Psellus' dialogue is laid. It relates also an instance of dæmoniacal possession which cannot be accounted for on the supposition that such possessions were imaginary.

The propriety of apprising the mere English reader of the distinction between a dæmon and the devil suggests itself here.[2] The

---

[1] Both terms refer to the same group of heretics called Euchitæ in Greek and called Massalians in Syriac, which translates as 'people of prayer'. They were founded late in the fourth century C.E., probably in Thrace. They believed in ecstatic communion with the Holy Ghost, although the orthodox churchmen of the time saw that as demonic possession. Psellus begins his book as a diatribe against the Euchitæ because of their supposed commerce with dæmons. Dimitri Obolensky in his book *The Bogomils* is of the opinion that Psellus only had a vague idea of the doctrines of the Euchitæ. Maybe Psellus introduced the heresies of the Euchitæ as a way of launching into a discussion of demons from a theologically respectable position. –Ed.

[2] Properly speaking, the Pagan mythology, though it taught a future state of punishment, had nothing analogous with the hell of [Christian] revelation. Neither Charon, nor Pluto, nor Æaens, nor Rhadamanthus [the gods and guides to the Greek underworld], thus bears the slightest resemblance to that apostate being who is variously designated Adversary, Tempter, and Traducer [i.e. the Devil]. The local arrangement, too, or the Pagan hell, and the administration of its punishments, essentially distinguished it from the hell of the Christian system. The Pagan hell was ludicrously divided into compartments, in which men were punished according to their respective demerits, and had, besides, attached a region called the Elysian Plains, to whence heroes (first-rate characters, in the Pagan's estimate) were admitted immediately on their decease, and minor offenders after they had undergone a purgatorial process. It is true the Latin Christians adopted the tern Inferni to express hell; yet that was rather because it was more convenient to adopt

Pagan world, for the most part, knew nothing whatever of the devil, though well acquainted with dæmons, and addicted to their worship; and nothing can be more clearly evinced from Scripture than the fact that there is but one devil, whereas the dæmons are numerous; the distinction between them, though invariably observed in Scripture, has not been carried out in either our authorized translation, the German of Luther, or the Geneva French [translation].[1] It has been rigidly preserved, however, by the Syriac version, all the Latin translations, ancient and modern, and Diodatti's Italian version. We cannot do better than cite what Dr. Campbell [2] has so lucidly written on this subject; after remarking that there is scarcely any perceptible difference between δαιμων [*daimon*] and δαιμονιον [*daimonion*], this acute critic observes (*Diss[ertations]*. vi. p. 1, § 8): —

"Δαιμονιον [*daimonion*], dæmon, occurs frequently in the Gospels, and always in reference to possessions, real or supposed; but the word διαβολος [*diabolos*], devil, is *never* so applied. The use of the term δαιμονιον, dæmon, is as constantly indefinite as the term δαιβολος, devil, is definite: not but that it is sometimes attended by the article, but that is only when the ordinary rules of composition require that the article be used of a term that is strictly indefinite. Thus when a possession is first named, it is called simply δαιμονιον [*daimonion*], or dæmon, or πνευμα αχαθαοτον [*pneuma achathaoton*], an unclean spirit; never το δαιμονιον [*to daimonion*], or το πνευμα αχαθαοτον [*to pneuma achathaoton*]; but when in the progress of the story mention is again made of the same dæmon, he is styled το δαιμονιον, the dæmon, namely, that already spoken of; and in English, as well as Greek, this is the usage in regard to all indefinites.

Further, the plural δαιμονια [*daimonia*] occurs frequently,

---

a term in general use, and which, in its widest signification, included the idea of a future state of punishment, than because there was much natural fitness in the term to convey the idea intended.

[1] This failure to distinguish the two different terms, and their uniform translation as 'devil' regardless of their original meaning, has caused more confusion, anguish, pain and suffering than perhaps any other mis-translation in the Bible - Ed.

[2] Dr George Campbell (1719-1796), *A Dissertation on Miracles.* – Ed.

applied to the same order of beings with the singular; but what sets the difference of signification in the clearest light is that though both words, διαβολος [*diabolos*] and δαιμονιον [*daimonion*], occur often in the *Septuagint*,[1] they are invariably used for translating different Hebrew words; διαβολος [*diabolos*] is always in Hebrew either צר *tsar*,[2] enemy, or שתן, Satan, adversary, words never translated δαιμονιον [*daimonion*]. This word [*daimonion*], on the contrary, is made to express some Hebrew term signifying [either] idol, Pagan deity, apparition, or what some render [as] satyr.

What the precise idea of the dæmons to whom possessions were ascribed then was, it would, perhaps, be impossible for us with any certainty to affirm; but as it is evident that the two words διαβολος and δαιμονιον are not once confounded, though the first occurs in the New Testament upwards of thirty times, and the second about sixty, they can by no just rule of interpretation be rendered by the same term; possessions are never attributed to the being termed ο διαβολος [*o diabolos*], nor are his authority and dominion ever ascribed to dæmons. Nay, when the discriminating appellations of the devil are occasionally mentioned, διαμονιον [*diamonion*] is never used as one.

It may be proper to subjoin here the most striking instances of the term being mistranslated in the authorized version [of the Bible].

Acts xvii., 18: "Others said he seemeth to be a setter forth, of *strange gods*," should be [translated as] strange dæmons.

1st Corinth[ians]. x., 20, 21: "The things which the Gentiles sacrifice they sacrifice to *devils*, and not to God, and I would not that ye should have fellowship with *devils*; ye cannot drink the cup of the Lord, and the cup of *devils*; ye cannot be partakers of the Lord's table and the table of *devils*." Here in every instance the word rendered

---

[1] The ancient Koine Greek translation of the Jewish Scriptures or Hebrew Bible translated in Alexandria between the third and first centuries BCE. Sometimes simply referred to as the 'LXX' in reference to the 70 scholars who are supposed to have laboured on the translation –Ed.

[2] Printed as ער in the first edition, but obviously mean to be צר.

devils should be rendered dæmons.

Rev[elation]. ix., 20: "The rest of the men which were not killed by these plagues, yet repented not of the works of their hands, that they should not worship *devils*;" read dæmons.

1st Tim[othy]. iv., 1: "Giving heed to seducing spirits, and doctrine of *devils*," should be dæmons.

James ii., 19: "Thou believest that there is one God; thou doest well; the *devils* also believe and tremble;" substitute dæmons.

With respect to the instance of dæmoniacal possession recorded in Psellus' work, and which is irreconcilable with the supposition that such possessions were imaginary, although, indeed, it may be objected that that particular case is not duly authenticated, yet we can hardly conceive it possible for any one who implicitly believes the infallible truth of Scripture, and reads it with ordinary attention, to call in question the reality of dæmoniacal possessions, at least in the apostolic age. Nothing can be more pertinent than Dr. Campbell's remarks on this subject (*Diss[ertations]*. vi., p. 1, § 10):—

"A late learned and ingenious author (Dr. Farmer)," observes Dr. Campbell, "has written an elaborate dissertation to evince that there was no real possession in the demoniacs mentioned in the Gospel, but that the style there employed was adopted merely in conformity to popular prejudice, and used of a natural disease. Concerning this doctrine, I shall only say, in passing, that if there had been no more to argue from sacred writ in favour of the common opinion than the name δαιμονιζομενος [*daimonizomenos*], or even the phrases δαιμονιον εχειν [*daimonion echein*], εκβαλλειν [*ekballein*], &c., [then] I should have thought his explanation at least not improbable; but, when I find mention made of the number of dæmons in particular possessions, their action so expressly distinguished from that of the man possessed, conversations held by the former in regard to the disposal of them after their expulsion, and accounts given how they were actually disposed of — when I find desires and passions ascribed peculiarly to them, and similitudes taken from the conduct which they usually observe, it is impossible for me to deny their existence, without admitting that the sacred historians were either deceived themselves in regard to them, or intended to deceive their readers. Nay, if they were faithful historians, this reflection, I am afraid, will strike still deeper."

Without consenting to all that Psellus advances on the origin, nature, modes of action, and occasional manifestation of dæmons, yet, believing implicitly the sacred Scriptures, we can have no more doubt of the existence of such beings than we have of our own. Dr. Campbell also observes, (*Diss[ertations]*. vi., p. 1, § 11):—

"Though we cannot discover with certainty, from all that is said in the Gospel concerning possessions, whether the dæmons were conceived to be the ghosts of wicked men deceased, or lapsed angels, or (as was the opinion of some early Christian writers, Iust. M. [St Justin Matyr] *Apol[ogia]*.

1) the mongrel breed of certain angels (whom they understood by *the sons of God*, mentioned in *Genesis*, ch[apter]. vi.,
2) and of *the daughters of men*, it is plain they were conceived to be malignant spirits.[1]

They [the malignant spirits] are exhibited as the causes of the most direful calamities to the unhappy person whom they possess — dumbness, deafness, madness, palsy, and the like. The descriptive titles given them always denote some ill quality or other; most frequently they are called πνευματα αχαθαοτα [*pneumata achathaota*], unclean spirits; sometimes πνευματα πονηοα [*pneumata poneoa*], malign spirits; they are represented as conscious that they are doomed to misery and torments, though their punishment be for a while suspended. 'Art thou come hither, βαστανασαι ημας [*Bastanasai emas*], to torment us before the time?' *Matt[ew]*. viii., 29."[2]

---

[1] "That the sons of God saw the daughters of men that they were fair; and they took them wives of all they chose…There were giants in the earth in those days; and also after that, when the sons of God came in unto [copulated with] the daughters of men, and they bare children to them…" *Genesis* 6:2,4. The children were the Nephilim. -Ed.

[2] Before moving on to more modern theological opinions about the nature of dæmons, it is worthwhile to quote one more Classical source. Calcidius (c. 300

Michael Psellus

Calmet [1] seems to be of opinion that the dæmons are identical with the apostate angels:[2] we cannot but believe that such as were connected with dæmoniacal possession were the same with the apostate angels, the more especially as we find not the remotest allusion to their origin as a distinct class, and as both they and the apostate angels are represented as destined to future torment. The possessed with dæmons at Gadara cry out, on our Lord's approach, "Art thou come to torment us *before the time*" (*Matt*[*ew*]. viii., 29) — whilst our Lord says, delivering the future judgment, "Depart ye cursed into everlasting fire, *prepared* for the devil and his angels:" from which passages it would appear that neither Satan nor the dæmons are yet enduring the extreme punishment prepared for them; indeed, the scriptural opinion appears to be that, as the devil

---

C.E.) wrote in his *Commentarius*, chapter 135, that: "So the definition of 'dæmon' will be as follows: a dæmon is a rational, immortal, sensitive [having the five senses], ethereal, living being taking care of men. It is a living being, because it is a soul using a body; rational [able to think], because it is prudent; immortal, because it does not change one body for another, but always uses the same; sensitive, because it reflects and no choice can be made without enduring desire; it is called ethereal because of its abode or the quality of its body [derived from the aether]; taking care of men by reason of the will of God, who has given [men] the dæmons as guards [guardians]. This same definition will also hold for the aerial dæmon, except that this dæmon abides in the air and the nearer it is to the earth, the more adapted [it is] to passion. The rest of the dæmons are neither so laudable nor so friendly, and they are not always invisible, but sometimes they can be observed, when they change into diverging shapes. They also clothe themselves in the shadowy forms of bloodless images, drawing with them the filth of a stout body, often also acting as the revengers of crimes and impiety according to the sanction of divine justice. They also very often hurt of their own accord; for they are touched by an earthly passion as a result of the vicinity of the earth and they have an excessive partnership with matter, which the Ancients called the wicked soul. Some men call those and similar dæmons in a strict sense the runaway [fallen or apostate] angels". See Boeft (1977), pages 38-39 where the translator uses 'demon' instead of 'dæmon'. In other words the dæmons act as intermediaries between man and heaven, just like the angels, with the crucial distinction that whilst angels are just messengers [the literal meaning of 'angel'], dæmons can take a semi-material form, act, guard, help or hinder man. –Ed.

[1] Dom Augustin Calmet (1672-1757) a French Benedictine monk and theologian who wrote much about demons. In 1746 he also wrote a treatise on Vampires. –Ed.

[2] The angels that rejected God and fell from heaven to become demons. –Ed.

walketh about like a roaring lion seeking whom he may devour, going to and fro in the earth, walking up and down in it, so his emissaries, the apostate angels, the dæmons, roam through every part of it, inflicting diseases, tempting to sin, and blasting physical as well as moral good.

If it be said that such a supposition is irreconcilable with the power and beneficence of the Divine Being, will those who make such objection venture to deny the existence of moral and physical evil? And if that be reconcilable with the power and beneficence of the Supreme, why may not the doctrine just laid down? Will it be said that such a supposition is irreconcilable with the immutability and permanency of the Divine laws? Will those who make such objection assert, that the superficial knowledge they may have acquired of nature's laws warrants them in saying that they understand the Divine laws? — Who can tell *all* the causes that lead to any one, even the most insignificant, event? — And who can tell but that the laws of nature, without our perceiving it, are controlled by dæmonic agency? We only see a few of the links — we cannot see all the links of the chain that lead to any one result.

It may be proper to examine here the Heathen notion of the word dæmon, by which means (*mutatis mutandis*)[1] we will be better able to understand its scriptural application. Its etymology conveys the idea either of an acute intelligence or of an appointed agent; but as these may exist separately, in distinct beings, or combined in the same being, it is obvious mere etymology cannot guide us to a safe conclusion in our enquiry.

Homer applies the epithet dæmons, in more than one instance, to the *dii majorum gentium*[2] (*Iliad*, v. 222); but whether he regarded the *dii majorum gentium* as an inferior order of beings, subordinate to a superior intelligence, or heroes advanced to this

---

[1] All other things being equal. –Ed.

[2] The 12 main Olympic gods of the ancient Greek pantheon, Jupiter, Juno, Minerva/Pallas, Vesta, Ceres, Neptune, Venus, Vulcanus, Mars, Mercury, Apollo, and Diana. Gods that you might have expected to be in the top twelve, such as Saturn, belong to the *Dii Selecti*. –Ed.

eminence, or merely applied this term as suitable, in its primary sense of an acute intelligence, to beings of the very first order, is somewhat doubtful. The scholiast seems to favour the view last mentioned (Hom[er]. *Iliad*. Cantab[ury], 1711, vers[e]. 222). We cannot but be persuaded that Homer considered all the gods and goddesses of human origin, and occasionally gave glimpses of his opinion on this point, though he dared not openly to avow his sentiments.

One very striking instance of this furtive way of insinuating his private opinions we have in the 22nd book of the *Iliad*, 74th line, where, speaking of a river in the Troade, he says, Ον Χανθον καλεουσι θεοι, ανδρες δε Σκαμανδρον, "which the Gods call Xanthus, but men Scamander;" [1] Xanthus being the name by which the ancients designated the river, he almost says that ancients and gods are convertible terms. It may be objected, "can Jupiter himself be included under this idea — Jupiter, to whom almighty power and supreme dominion are attributed, and who is styled by the poets "*the father of gods and men, the greatest and best of beings?*" De La Motte's reply to Madame Dacier [2] is here very apposite —

"What! Could Homer seriously believe Jupiter to be the creator of gods and men? Could he think him the father of his own father Saturn, whom he drove out of heaven, or of Juno, his sister and his wife, of Neptune and Pluto, his brothers, or of the nymphs who had charge of him in his childhood, or of the giants who made war upon him, and would have dethroned him, if they had been then arrived at the age of manhood? How well his actions justify the Latin epithets, *optimus, maximus*, most gracious, most mighty, so often given him, [as] all the world knows." (*De la Critique*, seconde partie, *Des Dieux*.)

---

[1] Xanthus was the Greek name for Scamander, a river god. It is possible that Xanthus was the god and Scamander the river near Troy, but it is not made clear in the *Iliad*. —Ed.

[2] In 1699 Madame Dacier published a scholarly translation of the *Iliad* with a preface which was a reply to Homer's critics. Later in 1713 Houdart de la Motte, a wit and versifier, published a more free-form translation of *Iliad* in verse. —Ed.

On the whole, we are rather inclined to think that Homer considered all gods (the *dii majorum gentium* not excepted) as dæmons of human original. Hesiod follows next in order of time; he seems decidedly of [the] opinion that all gods were dæmons, and originally human; he intimates that the dæmons are the men of the golden age, who lived *under Saturn*, and avers that they are the *protectors of mankind*, φυλαχας των θνητων ανθρωπων [*phylachas ton thneton anthropon*]. (Vide Scholiast on Homer's *Iliad*, A. 222.) Socrates' sentiments on this subject, as also those of Plato and his immediate disciples, may be gathered from the following extract from Plato's *Cratylus*: —

"*Soc*[*rates*]. What shall we consider next?

Hermogenes. Dæmons, to be sure, and heroes, and men.

Soc[*rates*]. Let it be dæmons, then, and with what propriety they are so named. Consider, Hermogenes, if I say ought worthy of your attention as to what might have been the sense of the word dæmon.

Hermog[*enes*]. Proceed.

Soc[*rates*]. Are you aware that Hesiod says certain [men] are dæmons?

Hermog[*enes*]. I don't remember it.

Soc[*rates*]. Nor that he says the first generation of men were golden?

Herm[*ogenes*]. I know that, at all events.

Soc[*rates*]. Well, then, he speaks thus respecting it: —

> 'When destiny concealed this generation
> They were called pure subterranean Intelligences [1] [*Daimones*],
> Excellent, Avertors of evils, Protectors of mortal men.'

Herm[*ogenes*]. What, then, pray?

Soc[*rates*]. I think he calls a generation the golden [generation], not as though produced from gold, but because excellent and glorious; and I

---

[1] We have rendered this word, δαιμονες [*daimones*], [as] intelligences, and will [do so] throughout. Were we to render it dæmons, it would be impossible to convey the agreeable play on the word which afterwards occurs.

conjecture it is for analogous reasons he says we are an iron generation.

Herm[*ogenes*]. You say the truth.

Soc[*rates*]. You think, then, he would say, if anyone of the present age were excellent, he belonged to the golden age?

Herm[*ogenes*]. It is but the natural inference.

Soc[*rates*]. Who are excellent but the wise?

Herm[*ogenes*]. The wise, none else.

Soc[*rates*]. This, therefore, he specially intimates respecting Intelligences, that he designated them Intelligences because [they are] wise and intelligent, and in our ancient speech the word occurs. Accordingly not only Hesiod, but many other poets also, calls them appropriately thus. How many, too, are in the habit of saying, when, a good man dies, that be obtains a glorious lot, and dignity, and becomes an intelligence, designating him thus owing to his wisdom? In the same manner I aver that the intelligent man is every good man, and that the same, whether living or dead, is intellectual, and is correctly called all intelligence." —

Plutarch,[1] who flourished in the second century, gives the following as his doctrine of dæmons: —

"According to a divine nature and justice, the souls of virtuous men are advanced to the rank of dæmons; if they are properly purified, they are exalted into gods, not by any political institution, but according to right reason." The same author says in another place (*de Isis et Osiris*, p. 361), that Isis and Osiris were for their virtue changed into gods, as were Hercules and Bacchus afterwards, receiving the united honours both of gods and dæmons.

From these data we conclude that the word dæmon, as signifying in its abstract sense an intelligence, was occasionally applied from the earliest times to deities of the very first order, but afterwards came to be appropriated to deified men; and that the

---

[1] Plutarch [46-120 C.E.] was a Neoplatonist, historian and essayist born near Delphi. —Ed.

heathen (philosophers excepted) believed in no being identical with or bearing the slightest resemblance to our [Christian] God. In the language of one who cannot be suspected of any partiality to Christianity, they were *"a kind of superstitious atheists, who acknowledged no being that corresponds with our idea of a deity."* (*Nat. Hist. of Rel.*, sect. iv.) [1]

The heathen did not pretend to be acquainted with all the existing dæmons or intelligences. So sensible were the Greeks of their ignorance on this head, that they actually had, in [St.] Paul's day, an altar at Athens with the inscription, "To an unknown God." They thought by this contrivance to obviate any bad results that might accrue from their ignorance, and secure to every dæmon or intelligence a due share of honour. Paul accordingly, with ingenious artifice, takes advantage of this circumstance to introduce Jesus to their notice as a dæmon [2] or intelligence they were unconsciously

---

[1] David Hume, *Natural History of Religion.* -Ed.

[2] It seems probable that the line of conduct pursued by the Apostle [Paul] on this occasion was suggested by the remark of the Athenians themselves, "*he seems to be a setter forth of strange intelligences*," (usually rendered dæmons); because he preached to them τον Ιμσουν και την Ανσατασιν, Jesus and Resurrection, they conceived Jesus to be a male intelligence, and Resurrection; Anastasin, [to be] a female intelligence, according to their custom deifying abstract qualities, and making them gods and goddesses as suited the gender of the name. Nor can this conduct of the Apostle be termed with any propriety "a pious fraud". 'Tis true that though the term dæmon in its primary use signifies intelligence, his auditors [listeners] would be very apt to take the term in its more extended sense. The Apostle, however, could not justly be held responsible for the acceptation in which they choose to take his words; yet it must be admitted that the Apostle did not in this instance state the whole truth, but merely so much as suited his immediate purpose of extricating himself from the power of their fanatical philosophers. His principal object seems to have been to show that on their own principles, which admitted a multiplicity of gods, and regarded without jealousy the gods of other nations, they could not in justice or consistency punish him for preaching a God they had never heard of before, even Jesus. With a similar tact the Apostle rescued himself from the malice of the Jews, when arraigned before the high priest, by avowing himself a Pharisee, and insisting that the doctrine of a future resurrection was the great matter of dispute; but this, as in the former instance, was not the whole truth; it answered, however, the Apostle's purpose by creating a division in his favour. Surely this was the wisdom of the serpent, without its venom.

worshipping. He thus apologizes on Mar's Hill, (*Acts* xvii. 21): —

"Ye men of Athens, I perceive that in every thing you somewhat *surpass in the worship* of dæmons (κατα παντα ως δεισιδαιμονεστερους [4]); for as I passed by, and beheld your devotions, I found an altar with this inscription, "*to an unknown God;*" whom therefore you *ignorantly worship*, Him declare I unto you:" In this apology the word dæmon does not convey the idea of either an impure or malignant being, but simply of an intelligence.

It can hardly be questioned but that the heathen, when worshipping deified men as dæmons, were really worshipping beings who had no existence but in their own imaginations; and in so doing, though they could not be said to worship any *particular dæmon*, yet might they with propriety be called worshippers or dæmons, beings which, whether real or imaginary, were confessedly inferior to the Supreme.[1] In this seems to lie the force of the Apostle's remark (*1st Cor*[*inthians*]. x., 19, 20,) "What say I, then? That the idol is anything, or that which is offered in sacrifice to idols anything? But I say that the things which the Gentiles sacrifice they sacrifice to dæmons, and not to God, and I would not that you should have fellowship with dæmons. Ye cannot drink the cup of the Lord, and the cup of dæmons!"

As if the Apostle had said, "do I mean to assert that an idol is *intrinsically* anything? By no means; the veriest tyro in the school of Christ knows that an idol is nothing, for eyes have they, and see not, &c.; but while I grant this, I still maintain that the things which the Gentiles sacrifice they sacrifice to dæmons, of which the idols are symbolical representations." Possibly the particular dæmon intended by the idol might have no existence, but idols may be considered with propriety to represent the class,

---

[4] The Athenians gloried in the fact that they were δεισιδαιμονεστερους [*deisidaimonesterons*] than the other states of Greece, and must have considered the Apostle's language highly complimentary.
[1] But infinitely more approachable. —Ed.

viz., beings intermediate between God and man, inferior to the former, but superior to the latter; "for to all who come under this description, real or imaginary, good or bad, the name dæmons (intelligences) is promiscuously applied.

The reality of such intermediate order of beings revelation everywhere supposes, and rational theism does not contradict. Now it is to the *kind* expressed in the definition now given that the pagan deities are represented as corresponding, and not individually to *particular dæmons*, actually existing. To say, therefore, that the Gentiles sacrifice to dæmons is no more than to say that they sacrifice to beings which, whether real or imaginary, we perceive, from their own account of them, to be below the Supreme." (Campb[ell], *Diss[ertation on Miracles]*. vi., p. 1, § 15.)

It may be asked, of what practical utility is a work of this nature — of what practical importance can it be whether we believe or disbelieve the existence of dæmons? We humbly conceive it is not optional with us to treat any portion of divine truth as unimportant, because we cannot see its practical bearing upon the conduct. If it can be unequivocally shown from the Word of God that dæmons exist, [then] the belief of the fact belongs to us, [and] the utility of it to Him that permits it.

At the same time, we cannot forbear observing that, if it be a work of utility to throw light, in the least degree, on any portion of the Word of God, and to rescue a term or a passage from a perverted use, then we flatter ourselves such ends may be in some measure effected by the publication of Psellus' work; but if there were no other reason for its publication than a desire to communicate the arguments with which, in those comparatively early times, men of a philosophic turn of mind fortified themselves in the belief of dæmoniacal possessions (as well in the Apostolic age as in their own time), we conceive none could justly condemn such a laudable motive. Surely a supercilious contempt for the Anakim[1] of ancient literature, which would censure them unheard, or consign their writings to oblivion, is no mark of either liberality or wisdom in the present age.

[Marcus Collisson]

---

[1] The Anakim were children of the 'Watchers' or Nephilim and the daughers of men. There is a tradition that their children lived into historical times and were kings or gods. –Ed.

MICHÆL PSELLUS' DIALOGUE,

BETWEEN

TIMOTHY AND THRACIAN,

ON THE OPERATION OF DÆMONS,

Versus Manes and the Euchitæ [1]

TIMOTHY. — Is it long, Thracian, since you visited Byzantium?

THRACIAN. — Yes, it is long, Timothy; two years perhaps, or more: I have been abroad.

TIMOTHY. — But where, and why, and engaged in what business, were you away so long?

THRACIAN. — The questions you put would take too long to answer just now; I must devise Alcinous' narrative [2] if I am obliged to particularize every thing I was present at, and every thing I endured, while constrained to associate with impious characters — those Euchitæ, or, as many call them, Enthusiasts [3] — have you not

---

[1] See note at the end of the book explaining the Manes and Euchitæ. This note was too large to form a regular footnote. Manes was the prophet Mani, executed in 276 C.E. for his dualistic and heretical views, which were partly the source of the doctrines of the Euchitæ. –Ed.

[2] *Alcinous' narrative.* — Ulysses, feasting with Alcinous, king of the Phœacians, presuming on the monarch's ignorance, amused himself at his expense by giving a fictitious narrative of his adventures amongst the Lotophagi, Lestrigons, and Cyclops. Hence any lying narrative, filled with marvellous adventures, came to be called Alcinous' narrative, *i.e.* such a narrative as was delivered for Alcinous' amusement by Ulysses. The phrase passed into a proverb, and is thus used by Plato, de *Repub[ublic]*., lib. x.

[3] It is likely that this is what Aleister Crowley had in mind when he wrote his essay on *Energised Enthusiasm*. –Ed.

heard of them at all?[1]

TIMOTHY. — Why, I understand that there are amongst us individuals as godless as they are absurd, and that in the midst of the sacred quire [2] (to speak in comedian style;) but as to their dogmas, their customs, their laws, their proceedings, their discourses, I have not yet been able to learn any thing about them; wherefore I beg of you to tell me most explicitly whatever you know, if you are disposed to oblige an intimate acquaintance, I will even add, a friend.

THRACIAN. — Even have it so, friend Timothy, though it be enough to give one a headache if he but attempt to describe the outlandish doctrines and doings of dæmonry; and though you cannot possibly derive any advantage from such description — for, if it be true what Simonides says, that the statement of facts is their delineation,[3] and that therefore the statement of profitable facts must be profitable, and the statement of unprofitable facts quite the opposite — what possible benefit could you derive from my delineating their seductive statements?

TIMOTHY. — Nay, but I shall be greatly benefited, Thracian; surely it is not unserviceable for physicians to be acquainted with drugs of a deadly nature, that so none may be endangered by their use: besides, some of the particulars, at all events, will not be unprofitable. We have our choice, therefore, either to carry off from your disquisition what is profitable, or to be on our guard of it if it have anything pernicious.

THRACIAN. — Agreed, my friend; you shall hear (as the poet says) truths certainly, but most unpleasant ones: but if my narrative advert [refers] to certain unseemly proceedings, I require of you, in common justice, not to be angry with me who relate them, but with those who

---

[1] The Euchitæ came from Thrace, so it is significant that one of the speakers is a Thracian, who can therefore be expected to know more about the Euchitæ than Timothy. —Ed.

[2] In holy orders.

[3] *The statement of facts is their delineation.* — The following is an expression not only of Simonides, but Democritus, λογος εργου σκιη, the narrative of a fact is its shadow.

do them. This execrable doctrine had its rise with Manes [1] the Maniac, from him their [the Euchitæ's] multitudinous origins have flowed down as from a fœtid fountain; for, according to the accursed Manes, [2] there were two origins of all things: he, with senseless impiety, opposed a god, the author of evil, to God, the Creator of every good — a ruler of the wickedness of the Terrestrials, to the bounteous Ruler of the Cœlestials.

But the dæmoniacal Euchitæ have adopted yet a third origin; according to them, two sons, with their father, make the senior and the junior origin; to the father they have assigned the supra-mundane region solely, to the younger son the atmospheric region, and to the elder the government of things in the world — a theory which differs in nothing from the Greek mythology, according to which the universe is portioned out into three parts. These rotten-minded men, having laid this rotten foundation, thus far are unanimous in their sentiments; but from this point are divided in their judgments into three parties: some yield worship to both sons, maintaining, that though they are at variance, yet that both are equally deserving of being worshipped, because they are sprung from one parent, and will yet be reconciled.

But others serve the younger son as being the governor of the superior region, which extends immediately over the earth; and yet they do not absolutely disdain the elder son, but are on their guard of him, as of one who has it in his power to do them injury; while the third party, who are further sunk in impiety, withdraw altogether from the worship of the celestial son, and enshrine in their hearts the

---

[1] Here there is obviously a play on the word Manes, which we have endeavoured to preserve in some measure in the translation; the Greek reads παρα Μανεντος του μανεντος [*para Manentos tou menentos*]: this description of punning is very ancient. The Jews, playing on the word Beelzebul, signifying God of Heaven, converted it into Beelzebub, God of the Dunghill, he being supposed the god of a fly, that delights in ordure.

[2] The Greek reads επηρατω [*eperato*], which signifies lovely; we cannot but think this either a typographical error, or an error of some transcriber, and that the word, in the original MS., was επαρατω [*eparato*], which signifies accursed: this view is countenanced by the Latin translators, employing, as the synonym, *intestabilis*.

earthly alone, even Satan[ael],[1] dignifying him with the most august names, as, the First-begotten, Estranged from the Father, the Creator of Plants and Animals, and the rest of the compound beings. Preferring to make suit to him who is the Destroyer and Murderer, gracious God! How many insults do they offer to the Celestial, whom they pronounce envious, an unnatural persecutor of his brother, (who administers judiciously the government of the world) and aver, that it is his being puffed up with envy [that] occasions earthquakes and hail and famine, on which account they imprecate on him, as well other anathemas, as in particular that horrible one!

TIMOTHY. — By what train of reasoning have they brought themselves to believe and pronounce Satan[ael] a son of God, when not merely the Prophetic Writings, but the Oracles of Divine Truth everywhere speak but of one son, and he that reclined on our Lord's bosom (as is recorded in the Holy Gospel), exclaims, concerning the divine λογος [logos], "the Glory as of the *Only-begotten* of the Father," whence has such a tremendous error assailed them?

THRACIAN. — Whence, Timothy, but from the Prince of Lies, who deceives the understandings of his witless votaries by such vain-glorious fiction, vaunting that he will place his throne above the clouds, and averring that he will be equal to the Highest; for this very reason he has been consigned to outer darkness: and when he appears to them, he announces himself the first-begotten son of God and creator of all terrene [earthly] things, [2] who disposes of

---

[1] The original Greek is Σατανᾳηλ Satanael, not Σατανασ Satan, here and in all subsequent mentions. The ending '-ael' or '-iel' in Hebrew mythology often indicated an angel, as 'El' was the divine suffix and one of the names of god. Psellus would have been aware of this, and used 'Satanael' advisedly. So here the translator might be doing Psellus an injustice. See the section on the Bogomils in the Introduction. —Ed.

[2] This, it must be admitted, is the true character of Satan, so far as regards his lying propensities; he was a liar from the beginning. "When he speaketh a lie he speaketh his own, for he is a liar, and his (the liar's) father." But whether there be an admixture of vanity with mendacity, or his lies be uttered purely with a view to deceive, is not so easily determined; yet certainly his mendacious address to the Messiah, "All this power will I give thee and the glory of them, for that is delivered

everything in the world, and by this means, following up the peculiar foible of each, cheats the fools, who ought to have considered him an empty braggart and the arch-prince of falsehood, and overwhelmed with ridicule his pompous pretensions, instead of believing everything he says, and suffering themselves to be led about like oxen by the nose. However, it will soon be in their power to convict him of being a liar, for if they insist on his making good his honeyed promises, he will turn out no better than the ass in lion's skin which, when it attempted to roar like a lion, its braying betrayed.

At present, however, they resemble the blind, and the deaf, and the insane, since they cannot perceive, from the consanguinity of universal nature, that there is but one Creator, nor hear that very consanguinity declaring the self-same truth, nor discover, by reasoning, that if there were two opposite creators, there would not be that *one* arrangement and *oneness* (ενωσις [*enosis*]) which binds all things together. As the Prophet says, "the ox and the ass know their master and their master's crib," but these bid their Master farewell, and have elected to the place of God the most abject of all creatures. "Scorched though they be with the fire," (as the Proverb says) they yet follow and precipitate themselves into that fire which has long been provided for him and his co-apostates.

TIMOTHY. — But what profit do they derive from abjuring the Divine religion received from their fathers,[1] and rushing on certain destruction?

---

unto me, and to whomsoever I will I give it," seems to partake of a boastful character.

[1] Here we see how little dependence can be placed on that faith which is founded on human authority, "which stands in the wisdom of man and not in the power of God." Those who can assign no better reason for their Christianity than that it was transmitted from their fathers, will become Pagans, Mahommedans, or Infidels, when they cannot exercise their religion safely, or when it is more conducive to their temporal interest to renounce it; or else they are liable to be drawn into any fanciful theory, that has but the charm of novelty to recommend it, with talent and eloquence to enforce it. Little dependence can be reposed in any faith which is not the result of an enlightened, rational conviction. Superstition itself is vastly more influential than nominal Christianity.

THRACIAN. — As to profit, I do not know that they derive any, but I rather think not; for though the dæmons promise them gold, and possessions, and notoriety, yet you know they cannot give them to any: they do, however, present to the initiated phantasms and flashing appearances,[1] which these men-detesters of God call visions of God. Such as wish to be spectators of them, gracious Heavens! How many shameful things, how many unutterable and detestable [things] must they witness! For everything which we consider sanctioned by law, and a doctrine to be preached, and a duty to be practised, they madly disregard, nay, they even disregard the laws of nature; to commit their debaucheries to writing would only befit the impure pen of Archilochus,[2] nay, I do think that were he present he would be loath to commemorate orgies so detestable and vile, as were never witnessed in Greece, no, nor in any barbarous land; for where or when did anyone ever hear that man, that august and sacred animal, ate excretions, whether moist or dry — a monstrosity which, I believe, not even wild beasts in a rabid state are capable of committing, and yet this is but the preliminary proceeding with these execrable wretches.

TIMOTHY. — What for, Thracian?

THRACIAN. — Oh, this is one of their secrets — they know best who do it: however, on my frequently questioning on this point, all I could learn was, that the dæmons became friendly and affable on their partaking of the excretions. In this particular I was satisfied they spoke truth, though incapable of speaking it in other matters; since nothing can be so eminently gratifying to hostile spirits as to see man (who is an object of envy), man who has been honoured with the Divine image, fallen to such a state of degradation: this is

---

[1] This wording has echoes of the phraseology of the *Chaldaean 35 Oracles.* –Ed.

[2] *The impure pen of Archilochus.* — Archilochus was paying his addresses to the daughter of one Lycambes, and was accepted as a suitor; but a richer candidate for the lady's hand presenting himself, [and] Archilochus was dismissed. Upon this Archilochus lampooned Lycambes in Iambic verse, and that with such effect that in a fit of vexation he [Lycambes] committed suicide. Horace, in his *Ars Poetica* (v. 79), in allusion to this circumstance, says:— "*Archilocum proprio rabies armavit Iambo.*"

putting the finishing stroke on their folly. Nor is this confined to the Antistites of the dogma [1] (to whom they tack the appellation, Apostles), but extends to the Euchitæ and the Gnosti.[2] But as to their

---

[1] It is remarkable that in the whole course of this treatise Psellus, speaking of the most revolting doctrines, never once employs the term αιρεσις [airesis], but δογμα [dogma], which his Latin translator improperly renders hæresis [heresy]. To what is this attributable? — are we to suppose that the word αιρεσις [airesis] was unknown to Psellus as a term of reproach, or that however appropriate the term might be to express the word 'sect', it was altogether inappropriate to express the doctrine of a sect. No one instance can be shown in Scripture, nor in the writings of the first two centuries, of an *opinion*, whether true or false, being denominated heresy. It is applied in Scripture indifferently to either a good or bad sect, without implying either favour or censure, (thus we read the sect of the Saducces, the sect of the Pharisees, the strictest sect of our religion), but never to a sentiment, whether good or bad; in fact, it is nearly synonymous with ζχισμα [schisma], rendered in the authorized version division, ζχισμα [schisma], being the incipient state of that which, in its more confirmed and aggravated form, is αιρεσις [airesis]. There is one passage in the New Testament which, to a superficial reader, might seem to clash with the views here stated. "A man that is a heretick after the first and second admonition reject; knowing that he who is such is subverted and sinneth, being condemned of himself" — (Tit[us]. iii, 10, 11). This is a mis-translation in two ways, for not only does it attach to the word αιρετικος [airetikos], a modern and ecclesiastical sense, which was unknown in primitive times, but it is at variance with the very genius and structure of the language. On this last point Dr. Campbell, with his usual acuteness and accuracy, observes (Diss[ertation on Miracles]. 9. p. 4. s. 11):— It is plain, from the genius of the language, that the word αιρετικος [airetikos] in this place does not mean a member of an αιρεςις [airesis] or sect, who may be *unconscious of any fault,* and so is not equivalent to our word sectary, much less does it answer to our English word heretic, which always implies one who entertains opinions in religion not only erroneous but pernicious; whereas we have shown that the word αιρεςις [airesis], in scriptural use, has no necessary connection with opinion at all; its immediate connection is with division or dissension, as it is thereby that sects and parties are formed. Ἀιρετικος ανθρωπος [airetikos anthropos] must therefore mean, one who is the founder of a sect, or at least has the disposition to create αιρεςεις [airesis] or sects in the community, and may properly be rendered a *factious man."*

[2] The Greek reads Γνωστοις [Gnostois], the Lat[in] Comment[ary] suggests Γνωστικοις [Gnostikois], the name of a well-known sect, but we conceive Γνωστοις [Gnostois] to be the correct reading, and that it is not the Gnostics are referred to, but a particular class among the Euchitæ; called Gnosti, or Litterati. The conclusion we would draw from the above passage is, that the Euchitæ were divided into three classes — the Proestatoi or Presidents, the Gnosti or Literati, and the Euchitæ or

mystical sacrifice,[1] God preserve me! who could describe it? I blush to repeat the shameful things I witnessed, and yet I am bound to repeat them, for you, Timothy, have already prevailed on me; I will therefore skim over them lightly, omitting the more shameful proceedings, lest I should seem to be acting a tragedy, [rather than giving a plain statement of facts.] [2]

Vesperi enim luminibus accensis, quo tempore salutarem domini celebramus passionem, in domum præscriptam deductis, quas sacrilegi sacris suis initiaverunt, puellis ne lucem execrandi quod designant, flagitii testem habeant, cum puellis libidinose volutantur in quamcumque tandem, seu sororem, seu propriam filiam, seu matrem quilibet inciderit. Siquidem et hac in re dæmonibus rem gratam facere arbitrantur, si leges divinas transgressi fuerint, in quibas cautum est, ne nuptiæ cum sanguine cognato contrahantur. [3]

Having perfected this rite, they are dismissed; on the expiry of nine months, when the unnatural progeny of an unnatural seed is about being born, they meet again at the same place, and on the third day after parturition, tearing the wretched infants from their mothers, and scarifying their tender flesh with knives, they catch in basins the dripping blood, and casting the infants, still breathing, on the pile, consume them; afterwards, mingling their ashes with the blood in the basins, they make a sort of horrible compound, with which, secretly defiling their food, liquid and solid, like those who mix poison with mead, not only they themselves partake of these viands, but others also who are not privy to their secret proceedings.[4]

TIMOTHY. — What end do they propose to themselves by such

Praying-men, who formed perhaps the uneducated and largest portion — the last being most generally known, and the most numerous, the whole body might have been called by the general name, Euchitæ.

[1] This expression the Euchitæ derived from the Christians, who designated the Lord's Supper the mystical, i.e., symbolical sacrifice. This seems to indicate that Transubstantiation [of bread and wine] formed no part of the primitive creed.

[2] NOTE. — Wherever brackets are supplied thus [ ] the words included are not the author's, but are merely inserted to make the sense more explicit.

[3] Basically a description of various incestuous sexual relationships.

[4] This sounds like the worst kind of Christian propaganda against the Euchitæ, which was seen as fair game, being a heretical sect. –Ed.

revolting pollutions?

THRACIAN. — They are persuaded that by this means the divine symbols inscribed in our souls are thrust out and expunged, for so long as they continue there the dæmon tribe are afraid and keep aloof, as one might from the royal signet attached to a cabinet; in order, therefore, to enable the dæmons to reside in their souls they, without any apprehension, chase away the divine symbols, by their insults to heaven — and a profitable exchange they have made of it. But not satisfied with perpetrating this wickedness themselves, they lay a snare for others; the polluted viands tempting the pious also, who, without being aware of it, partake of the strange food, they like so many Tantali [1] serving up their children for the entertainment. [2]

TIMOTHY. — Good Heavens, Thracian! This is what my grandfather by the father's side predicted; for once being distressed, because some subverted as well the other privileges of the good as their acquisition of a liberal education,[3] I asked him, will there ever be a restoration? He being then an old man and very sagacious in foreseeing coming events, gently stroking my head and fetching a heavy sigh, replied,

"My son, my child, do you imagine that they will ever again restore literature, or anything excellent? The time is at hand when men will

---

[1] Tantalus served up his children at a banquet he prepared for the gods, and for this crime he was condemned to spend all eternity in Hades, with food and drink kept just tantalisingly out of his reach. –Ed.

[2] Query — might not that aversion which many of the Roman and Corinthian converts [to Christianity] evinced to partaking of food served up at entertainments, or exposed for sale by heathens, have been occasioned partly by a suspicion that it was secretly defiled by similar practices to what are here described.

[3] Here there seems a pointed allusion to the Emperor Julian [the last pagan Roman Emperor], whose artful policy it was to shut up the schools of the Christians, in which they taught philosophy and the liberal arts. It may indeed be objected that Julian lived in the fourth century, whereas Psellus flourished in the eleventh century. We are not, however, under any necessity for supposing that Psellus' *Dialogue* is laid for his own day. The Euchitæ, against whom this dialogue is levelled, started up at the close of the fourth century.

live worse than wild beasts, for now Antichrist [1] is at hand, even at the doors, and evil precursors in the shape of monstrous doctrines and unlawful practices, no better than the orgies of Bacchus, must usher in his advent. And whatever things have been represented by the Greeks in their tragedies, as Saturn and Thyestes [2] and Tantalus devouring their offspring, Œdipus debauching his mother, and Cinyras [3] his daughters, all these fearful enormities will break in upon our state; but see my son, and be on your guard, for know, know for certain, that not only individuals from the illiterate and unpolished class, but many also of the learned,[4] will be drawn away into the same practices." These things, if I am to judge from the result, he spoke prophetically; but I, when I recall to mind his words, which are as fresh in my memory now as when he uttered them, am surprised at what you tell me.

THRACIAN. — And well you may be surprised; for, many as are the absurd nations described by historians in the far North, and the parts about Lybia and Syrtes, yet I venture to say no one has ever heard of such impiety being practised by them, no, nor by the Celts, nor by any other nation near Britain, though [it is] destitute of laws and in a savage state.

TIMOTHY. — It is afflicting to think, Thracian, that such horrible practices should take up their abode in our quarter of the world. But a perplexity of long standing respecting dæmons distresses me; among other things, I should like to know whether they are manifestly seen by the dæmoniacal wretches [who evoke them].

THRACIAN. — Not a doubt of it, my friend, for this [result] they all

---

[1] An being who resembles Christ but does not give true salvation, who appears close to the end-time, as mentioned in *Revelations*. –Ed.

[2] Atreus cooked and served Thyestes' sons to him. –Ed.

[3] King of Cyprus, son of Apollo. –Ed.

[4] It is somewhat remarkable that heresy (we use the word in its present acceptation) has always originated with the learned. We doubt if there can be adduced a single instance of an illiterate heresiarch [founder of a heresy], which would seem to show that its rise is not owing so much to the ignorance of the multitude as to a daring spirit of innovation and depraved ambition in men of learning.

strive, [with] might and main; [for] their assemblage and sacrifice, and rites, and every horrible practice of theirs, are held for this purpose, to bring about a manifestation.

TIMOTHY. — How then can they, being incorporeal, be seen with the visual organs?

THRACIAN. — But, my good friend, they are not incorporeal; the dæmon tribe have a body, and are conversant with corporeal beings, which one may learn even from the holy fathers of our religion, if one only addict himself heartily to magical practices. We hear many too relating how the dæmons appeared to them in a bodily form; and the divine Basilius,[1] who beheld invisible things (or at least not clear to ordinary eyes) maintains it, that not merely the dæmons, but even the pure angels have bodies,[2] being a sort of thin, aërial, and pure spirits; and in proof of this he adduces the testimony of David, most celebrated of the prophets, saying, "He maketh his angels spirits, and his messengers a flame of fire."[3] And it must needs be even so, for

---

[1] St. Basil (330-379 C.E.) bishop of Caesarea. —Ed.

[2] That Cœlestial beings, Messengers of God to men, have appeared in visible form, must be admitted by every believer in Revelation; but whether they appeared in their proper nature, or in a form suited to the specific occasion of appearance, it is difficult perhaps to determine; yet, if as the Apostle says, "there is a spiritual as well as a natural body, (*1st Cor[inthians]* xv., 44,) a body which shall neither be frail, nor gross, nor subject to the wants that oppress the present body, but one which shall be fitted for the highest possible spiritual service and happiness, there is nothing irrational in the supposition that angels may have such a body. Abstractedly considered, matter has nothing contaminating in it — nothing which morally unfits it for union with a pure spirit; it is merely owing to its being associated with fallen man, that it seems to possess a degrading property. The fact that the believer's happiness will not be consummated till the union of the soul and body at the resurrection, when the soul will occupy the body, not as a prison house, but as a suitable mansion, goes far to establish this latter point.

[3] This passage, Dr. Chalmers in one of his works, (we believe his *Astronomical Discourses*,) renders, "He maketh the winds his messengers, the flaming fire his servants." We cannot but consider the passage correctly rendered in the authorised version, "He maketh his angels spirits, [or winds], his ministers a flame of fire;" certain it is, unless we take the passage in this way, it will be utterly destitute of force and meaning, in the 1st chap[ter of] *Epist[le to the] Hebrews*, 7th verse, where the Apostle contrasts the superior power and authority of the Son with that of angels.

when the ministering spirits are despatched to their respective employments [1] (as the divine Paul says) they must needs have some body, in order to their moving, becoming stationary and apparent; for these effects could not be accomplished otherwise than through the medium of a body.

TIMOTHY. — How comes it then, that in most passages of Scripture they are spoken of as incorporeal.

THRACIAN. — It is the practice both with Christian and profane authors, even the most ancient, to speak of the grosser description of bodies as corporeal; but those which are very thin, eluding both the sight and touch, not only we Christians, but even many profane authors think fit to call incorporeal.

TIMOTHY. — But tell me, the body which angels have by natural constitution, is it the same with that which dæmons have?

THRACIAN. — What folly! There must be a vast difference, for the angelic, emitting a sort of extraneous rays, is oppressive and intolerable to the visual organs: but as to the dæmonic, whether it was once of this sort I cannot say, but so it would seem; (for Esaias [Isaiah] disparagingly calls Lucifer "him that had fallen") now, however it is an obscure and darksome sort of thing, saddened in aspect, divested of its kindred light; but the angelic nature is immaterial, and therefore is capable of penetrating and passing through all solids, being more impalpable than the sun's rays, which, passing through transparent bodies, the opaque objects on this earth reflect, so as to render its stroke endurable, for there is something material in it; but nothing can interpose opposition to an angel, because they present opposition to nothing, not being homogeneous with any thing; on the other hand, the bodies of dæmons, though constituted indistinct by their tenuity; are yet in some measure material and palpable.

TIMOTHY. — I am becoming quite a sage, Thracian, (as the proverb

---

[1] The passage referred to, plainly is, "are they not all ministering spirits sent forth to minister to those who shall be heirs of salvation."

says),[1] by these novel accessions of knowledge; for to me, indeed, this is a novel fact, that some dæmons are corporeal and palpable.

THRACIAN. — There is no novelty in our being ignorant of many things, so long as we are men, Timothy, as the saying is; 'tis well, however, if, as ages advance, our good sense increases. Be assured of this, that in making these statements, I am not uttering lying rhapsodies, like the Cretans: and Phœniceans,[2] but am persuaded of their truth from the Saviour's words, which affirm, that the dæmons shall be punished with fire, a punishment they would be incapable of if incorporeal. Since a being that is destitute of a body cannot suffer in the body, therefore they must needs undergo punishment by means of bodies, constituted capable of suffering. Much, however, I have suppressed which I heard from some who adventured themselves to intuition;[3] for my own part, I have never seen a being of that nature — Heaven grant that I may never behold the fearful looks of dæmons!

But I conversed with a monk in Mesopotamia, who really was an initiated inspector of dæmonic phantasms: these magical practices he afterwards abandoned as worthless and deceptive, and having made his recantation, attached himself to the true doctrine, which we profess, and assiduously applying himself, underwent a course of instruction at my hands; he accordingly told me many and extraordinary things about dæmons; and once, on my asking, if dæmons were capable of animal passion, "Not a doubt of it," said he.

Quemadmodum et sperma nonnulli eorum emittunt et vermes quosdam spermate procreant. At incredible est, inquam excrementi quicquam

---

[1] The following is an expression of Solon: γηρασχω δ' αει πολλα διδασχομενος, "I become old by constantly learning much," and seems to be the proverb alluded to.

[2] The Cretans and Phœnicians were remarkable for their lying propensities, so much so that their bad faith became proverbial. The Apostle Paul in the *Epistle to Titus*, (ch[apter] i. 12,) cites the Poet Epimenides description of them, with approbation of its truth, "the Cretans are always liars, evil beasts, slow bellies." — Every one has heard of the *Punica fides*. [The Carthaginians were famous for their great treachery].

[3] This is a technical phrase. See note on the words 'ridiculous tricks', in the 47th page. [now page 74 – Ed].

dæmonibus inesse, vasave spermatica et vitalia vasa quidem eis, inquit me, hujusmodi nulla insunt, superflui autem seu excrementi nescio quid emittunt hoc mihi asserenti credito. [1]

But, said I, if they derive nourishment, they must derive it as we do? Marcus [for that was his name], replied, some derive it by inhalation, as for instance a spirit resident in lungs and nerves, and some from moisture, but not as we do, with the mouth, but as sponges and testaceous[2] fishes do, by drawing nourishment from the extraneous moisture lying around them, and they afterwards void [give out] a spermatic substance, but they do not all resemble each other in this particular, but only such descriptions of dæmons as are allied to matter, such as the Lucifugus,[3] and Aqueous, and Subterranean. And are there many descriptions of dæmons, Marcus, I asked again? There are many, said he, and of every possible variety of figure and conformation, so that the air is full of them, both that above and that around us, the earth and the sea are full of them, and the lowest subterranean depths. Then, said I, if it would not be troublesome, would you particularize each? It would be troublesome, said he, to recall to mind matters I have dislodged from thence, yet I cannot refuse, when you command, and so saying he counted off many species of dæmons, adding their names, their forms, and their haunts.

TIMOTHY. — What's to hinder you then Thracian, enumerating them to us?

THRACIAN. — I was not very solicitous, my good sir, to retain either the substance or arrangement of that conversation, nor can I now recollect it. What possible benefit could I derive from an over-solicitude to retain their names, their, haunts, and in what particular they resemble, and in what differ from each other? Therefore, I have allowed such insipid matter to escape my memory, yet, I retain a little out of a great deal, and whatever you are curious about, if you enquire of me you shall know it.

---

[1] About the eating of excrement.
[2] Shellfish and others having a hard shell. —Ed.
[3] Demons who "flee the light". —Ed.

TIMOTHY. — This in particular I wish to know, how many orders of dæmons are there?

THRACIAN. — He said, there were in all six species of dæmons, I know not whether subdividing the entire genus by their habits, or by the degree of their attachment to bodies — be that as it may, he said that the sexade [sixfold classification of dæmons] were corporeal and mundane, because in that number all corporeal circumstances are comprised, and agreeably to it the mundane system was constituted; afterwards he observed, that this first number [the sexade] was represented by the scalene triangle,[1] for that beings of the divine and celestial order were represented by the equilateral triangle, as being consistent with itself, and with difficulty inclinable to evil, whilst human beings were represented by the isosceles triangle,[2] as being in some measure liable to error in their choice, yet capable of reformation on repentance. On the other hand, that the dæmonic tribe were represented by the scalene [3] triangle, as being at variance with itself, and not at all approaching to excellence.

Whether he were really of this opinion or not, this is certain, he counted off six species of dæmons, and first he mentioned [the] Leliurium,[4] speaking in his barbarous vernacular tongue, a name which signifies Igneous. This order of dæmons haunts the air above

---

[1] A triangle with three unequal sides, and therefore representing the imperfect. –Ed.

[2] A triangle with two sides and two angles equal. –Ed.

[3] Here Ethics and Mathematics are curiously blended, few of our modern mathematicians, we believe, are in the habit of assigning a moral meaning to Geometrical problems, theorems, or figures; most probably this notion was derived from the Pythagoreans, but at all events, it shows that those who embraced such fanciful opinions were not the illiterate vulgar. It may be necessary to explain this conceit, more particularly to the mere English reader — the equilateral triangle, which was bounded by three equal sides, was considered the emblem of excellence, hence the celestial beings were regarded as represented by it. The Isosceles triangle, which was bounded by two equal and one unequal side, was considered not quite so perfect in its conformation, and was therefore supposed to represent human beings, while the Scalene triangle, which was bounded by three sides, every one of which was unequal to the other, was thought aptly to shadow forth the perverseness and waywardness or the dæmonic tribe.

[4] Query, is this the Lemures of the Latins, and the Leprechaun of the Irish.

us, for the entire genus has been expelled from the regions adjacent to the moon, as a profane thing with us would be expelled from a temple, but the second occupies the air contiguous to us, and is called by the proper name Aërial; the third is the Earthly, the fourth the Aqueous and Marine, the fifth the Subterranean, and the last the Lucifugus, which can scarcely be considered sentient beings.

All these species of dæmons are haters of God, and enemies of man, and they say, that the Aqueous and Subterranean are worse than the merely bad, but that the Lucifugus are eminently malicious and mischievous, for these, said he, not merely impair men's intellects, by fantasies and illusions, but destroy them with the same alacrity as we would the most savage wild beast. The Aqueous suffocate in the water all that approach them; the Subterranean and Lucifugus, if they can only insinuate themselves into the lungs of those they meet, seize and choke them, rendering them epileptic and insane; the Aërial and Earthly, with art and cunning stealthily approach and deceive men's minds, impelling them to unlawful and unnatural lusts.

But how, said I, or what doing [what], do they accomplish this? Is it by lording it over us, and leading us about wherever they please, as if we were so many slaves? Not by lording it over us, says Marcus, but by leading us into reminiscences, for when we are in an imaginative spirit, approaching by virtue of their spiritual nature, they whisper descriptions of sensual delights and pleasures, not that they actually emit distinct sounds, but they insinuate a sort of murmur, that serves with them the place of words. But it is impossible, said I, they could utter words without sound?

It is not impossible, said he, as you will perceive, if you only reflect, that when one is speaking to another at a distance, he must speak in a high key, but if he be near, he need barely murmur, and whisper into the ear of his auditor [listener], and if one could approach the very essence of the soul, there would be no occasion for any sound whatever, but any word we pleased would reach its destination by a noiseless path; a faculty which they say is possessed by disembodied spirits, for they bold communication with each other in a noiseless manner, in the same way the dæmons hold communication with us, without our perceiving it, so that it is impossible to discover from what quarter an attack may be made upon us.[1]

You need have no doubt on this point, if you only consider what happens in the atmosphere; when the sun shines, he combines colours and forms, and transmits them to objects capable of receiving them, (as we may observe in mirrors); thus also the dæmons, assuming appearances and colours, and whatever forms they please, transport them into our animal spirit, and occasion us in consequence a vast deal of trouble, suggesting designs, reviving the recollection of pleasures, obtruding representations of sensual delights, both waking and sleeping; sometimes, too, rousing the baser passions by titillations, they excite to insane and unnatural amours, and especially when they find warm perspirations co-operating; for in this way, donning Pluto's helmet,[2] with craft and the most refined subtlety, they create a commotion in men's minds.

The other description of dæmons have not a particle of wit, and are incapable of cunning, yet are they dangerous and very terrible, injuring after the manner of the Charonean spirit, for (as they report)

---

[1] This is indeed "the doctrine of dæmons," in all its length, depth, breadth, and fullness. Were one engaged [in] sinking a well, and life became suddenly extinct, by inhaling choke-damp, [then] his death was occasioned by one of the Lucifugus or Subterranean dæmons; was one while bathing to be suddenly seized with cramp, and sink to rise no more, [then] he was pulled under by one of the Aqueous or Marine dæmons; was one from not keeping the hands or the head industriously employed, to be haunted with the filthy vagrancies of a prurient imagination, [then] this was the work of an Aërial dæmon, whispering impure desires into his soul; so that, as Thracian says, "it was impossible to tell from what quarter an attack might be made upon us." How wretched must have been the condition of those enslaved to such a degrading superstition. Well might Horace ask (who probably spoke from a personal experience of this horrible slavery) —

Somnia terrores magicos, miracula, sagas
Nocturnos lemurs, portentaque Thessalia rides?
       Epist[le] II., book 2, v. 209, 210.

[2] Pluto's helmet conferred invisibility. It was given to him by the one-eyed giant Cyclops.

the Charonean spirit [1] destroys every thing that comes in its way, whether beast, man, or bird; in the same way these dæmons terrifically destroy everyone they fall in with, injuring them in body and mind, and subverting their natural habits; sometimes they destroy not merely men, but even irrational animals, in the fire, in the water, or by casting them over precipices. [2]

TIMOTHY. — But what can be their object in entering irrational animals? For this happened to the swine, at Gargasa [3] (as the Sacred Writings attest). I am not surprised if, being hostile to men, they injure them; but what is the sense of their entering irrational animals? [4]

THRACIAN. — Marcus said that it was not from any motive of hatred, nor from any hostile intention, that they pounced upon some beasts, but from a vehement desire for animal heat; for, as they inhabit the most profound depths, which are cold to the last degree, and destitute of moisture, they are excessively cold; being contracted and pained in consequence, they naturally long for a moist and vivifying heat to revel in, and spring into irrational animals, and

---

[1] Associated with caves and the Underworld. –Ed.

[2] A reference to Christ driving out demons in Gadarenes, which subsequently lodged in swine, and which then conveniently threw themselves over a precipice. – Ed.

[3] Presumably Gerasene or Gadarenes. See *Mark* 5:1-20: "And they came over unto the other side of the sea [of Galilee], into the country of the Gadarenes. And when he [Jesus] was come out of the ship, immediately there met him out of the tombs a man with an unclean spirit. Who had his dwelling among the tombs; and no man could bind him, not [even] with chains …neither could any man tame him…And all the devils besought him, saying, Send us into the swine, that we may enter into them. And forthwith Jesus gave them leave. And the unclean spirits went out, and entered into the swine: and [then] the herd ran violently down a steep place into the sea…and were choked in the sea." –Ed.

[4] The point of choosing to enter into irrational animals was that they feared Jesus would cast them into water, in the same way Solomon had used water to control demons. *Luke* 8:31: "And they [the demons] besought him [Jesus] that he would not command them to go out into the deep". But Jesus tricked them, by allowing them to enter into the herd of 2000 swine, and then compelling the animals to throw themselves into the sea, thereby neatly accomplishing what the demons had most feared. –Ed.

plunge into baths and pits; on the other hand, the heat that proceeds from fire they avoid, because [it is] consuming and scorching, but gladly attach themselves to the moisture of animals, as being congenial to their nature, but especially to that of man, as being most congenial of all; and when infused into them they occasion no small uproar, the pores in which the animal spirit resides being clogged, and the spirit confined and displaced by the bulk of their bodies, which is the cause of their agitating men's persons, and injuring their faculties, and obstructing their motions.

When a subterranean dæmon assails one, he agitates and distorts the person possessed, and speaks through him, using *the tongue of the sufferer* [1] as if it were his own member; but if a *lucifugus* dæmon clandestinely possess a person, it occasions a relaxation of his whole system, stops his utterance, and almost leaves the sufferer dead; for this last species is more allied to earth than the others, and is therefore excessively cold and dry, and anyone it can secretly possess, it blunts and obscures all the sufferer's natural power; but, because it is irrational and totally devoid of intellect, being governed by irrational whim, it has no more dread of reproof than the most intractable wild beast, for which reason it is designated with great propriety dumb and deaf; nor can a sufferer be dispossessed but by

---

[1] Potter, describing the three different kinds of *theomancers*, has a passage which throws considerable light on the above:-"One sort of *theomancers* were possessed with prophesying dæmons, which lodged within them, and dictated what they should answer to those who inquired of them, or spoke out of the bellies or breasts of the possessed persons, they all the while remaining speechless, and not so much *as moving their tongues or their lips;* or pronounced the answer themselves, *making use of the members* of the dæmoniac; these were called δαιμονιληπτοι [*daimonileptoi*], *i.e.* possessed with dæmons; and because the spirits either lodged or spoke within their bodies, they were also named εγγαστριμυθοι [*eggastrimnthoi*] (which name was also attributed to the dæmons). It is in allusion to such possessed persons Isaias [Isaiah] says, as the *Septuagint* have it, "If they say unto you, seek unto those whose speech is in their belly, and that speak out of the earth, those that utter vain words, that speak from the stomach, shall not a nation seek unto their God? Why do they inquire concerning the living from the dead?" ([John] Potter's [*Archaeologia Graeca, or the*] Antiq[*uities of Greece*], vol. i., 352, edit[ion] Edin[burgh], 1832.)

divine power, procurable by prayer and fasting.[1]

"But, Marcus," said I, "physicians would persuade us to be of another way of thinking, for they assert that such affections are not produced by dæmons, but are occasioned by an excess or deficiency of humours, or by a disordered state of the animal spirits, and accordingly they endeavour to cure them by medicine or dietetical regimen, but not by incantations or purifications."

Marcus replied — "It is not at all surprising if physicians make such an assertion, for they understand nothing but what is perceived by the senses, their whole attention being devoted to the body. Lethargies, Syncopes,[2] cases of hypochondriasm, delirium, which they can remove by vomits, or evacuations, or unguents,[3] it is quite correct to say that there are the effects of disordered humours; but enthusiasms, and madness, and possessions, with which when one is seized he is incapable of making any use of his judgment, his tongue, his imagination, his senses, it is quite another thing [that] moves and excites them, and speaks what the person seized is unconscious of uttering, though occasionally be prophesies something." With what propriety [I ask] can these effects be called the disordered movements of matter?

TIMOTHY. — How now, Thracian! do you yourself assent to what Marcus says?

THRACIAN. — Most undoubtedly, Timothy; for how could I do otherwise, when I recollect what the holy Gospels relate concerning persons possessed with dæmons, and what befell the man of Corinth at Paul's command,[4] and how many wonderful things are related of them by the [Church] Fathers; and moreover saw with my own eyes, and heard with my own ears, their doings at Elason; for a man in

---

[1] Our Lord says, in reference to the expulsion of dæmons, "This kind goeth not forth but by prayer and fasting." To this declaration allusion is here evidently made.
[2] Loss of consciousness, fainting. –Ed.
[3] From this we learn that the application of unguents to the sick, referred to by the Apostle James, was not a religious, but a purely medical application.
[4] Paul commanded that the man of Corith who had committed incest should be excommun-icated. –Ed.

that place was in the habit of delivering oracles after the manner of the priests of Phœbus,[1] and, amongst other things, predicted not a few concerning myself. Having collected the multitude of the initiated around him, he said —

"I apprise the present company of the fact that an individual will be sent against us, by whom the mysteries of our worship will be persecuted, and the mysteries of our service abolished; myself and many others shall be apprehended by that person; but, though he be very anxious to carry me off a prisoner to Byzantium, he shall not do it — not though he make many and vigorous efforts to accomplish it."

Such predictions he uttered, though I had never gone as far from the city as to the neighbouring villages. He described, too, my aspect, deportment, and occupation, and many who used to pass to and fro told me the facts. At length, when I did apprehend him, I asked him how he came to be gifted with the prophetic art? He, though he did not wish to divulge the secret, yet, labouring under a laconic necessity, confessed the truth, for he said that he had come to the knowledge of dæmoniacal practices through a certain vagabond African, who, bringing him by night to a mountain, causing him to partake of a certain herb, spitting into his mouth, and anointing his eyes with a certain unguent, enabled him to see a host of dæmons, from among which he perceived a sort of raven fly towards him, and down his throat into his stomach.[2]

From that time up to the present moment he could predict, but only respecting such things, and at such times, as the dæmon who possessed him wished; but on Passion week [3] and the Resurrection day, so much venerated by Christians, not though be himself should greatly desire it, is the dæmon who possessed him disposed to suggest anything.

These things he told me, and, when one of my followers struck him

---

[1] The sun god. –Ed.

[2] Similar to the shamanic experiences reported by Carlos Casteneda. –Ed.

[3] The days just before and just after the Easter crucifixion of Jesus are called Passion Week. –Ed.

on the cheek, "you," said he, "for this one blow shall receive many; and you," said he, turning to me, "shall, suffer great calamities in your person, for the dæmons are fearfully incensed against you for subverting their service, and will involve you in harassing dangers, such as you cannot by any possibility escape, unless some power superior to that of dæmons extricate you.[1] These things the polluted wretch predicted, as if uttering oracles from the Delphic Tripod; for they all happened, and I have been almost undone by the numerous dangers which beset me; from which my Saviour alone wonderfully rescued me; but who that has seen the oracle in which dæmons play upon wind instruments,[2] will say that madness in all its forms are

---

[1] This is just the oracular style. There was always some proviso attached to oracular responses, or some ambiguity in them, which was calculated to save the oracle's credit. Thus when Crœsus applied to Apollo's oracle at Delphos, to know whether he should march against Cyrus, he received for answer —

"*Crœsus Halym penetrans, magnam pervertet opum vim.*"
"If Crœsus cross the river Halys, he shall overturn a great empire."

The event proved [to be] his own overthrow. The same ambiguity attends the famous reply of the same oracle to Pyrrhus: —

"*Aio te Æacida, Romanos vincere possum.*"
"I do pronounce that Rome Pyrrhus shall overcome."

Which may be interpreted to mean, either that Rome should overcome Pyrrhus, or that Pyrrhus should overcome Rome. It is in much the same prudential spirit our hero of Elason here adds, "unless some power superior to the dæmons extricate you."

[2] This is a passage on which we confess ourselves utterly unable to throw any light; we scarcely dare to hazard a conjecture. It strikes us, however, that a very successful imposture might be played off by means of Æolian harps. Perhaps it is to something of that nature allusion is made. We may observe, by the way, it is a great mistake to suppose that oracles ceased universally on the coming of Christ (as what is here mentioned proves). Though daily declining, they continued long after, as the laws of the Emperors Theodosius [378-395 and 408-450 C.E.], Gratian [407 C.E.], and Valerian [253-260 C.E.] against such as consulted them clearly evince. It would be more proper to say that wherever the power of Christ was brought to bear upon them they ceased, and eventually died out. Their cessation is attested by Strabo, Juvenal, Lucan, and others. Plutarch accounts for it by saying that the benefits of the Gods are not eternal, as themselves, or that the genii who presided over oracles are subject to death; whilst Athanasius tells the Pagans they have been witnesses themselves that the sign of the cross puts the dæmons to flight, silences oracles, and

but the vitiated movements of matter?

TIMOTHY. — I am not at all surprised, Thracian, that physicians are of this way of thinking, for how many cannot at all understand this sort of thing? For my part, I was first of their opinion, until I saw what was absolutely portentous and monstrous in its character, which, as it is quite apropos to the present topic, I shall relate. An old man like me, and who has, besides, assumed the monastic habit, is incapable of telling a falsehood. I had an elder brother married to a woman, who was on the whole of a good disposition, but exceedingly perverse; she was, too, afflicted with a variety of diseases. She, in her confinement, was very ill, and raved extravagantly, and, tearing her bed gown, muttered a sort of barbarous tongue, in a low murmuring tone; nor could the bystanders comprehend what she said, but were in a state of perplexity, not knowing what to do in so desperate a case. Some women, however (for the sex is very quick in discovering expedients, and particularly clever in meeting exigencies),[1] fetched a very old bald-headed man, with his skin wrinkled and sun-burnt to a very dark hue, who, standing with his sword drawn beside the bed, affected to be angry with the invalid, and upbraided her much in his own tongue; (I mention that, because he was an Armenian).[2]

The woman replied to him in the same tongue; first she was very bold, and, leaning on the bed, [be]rated him with great spirit; but when the foreigner was more liberal with his exorcisms, and, as if in a passion, threatened to strike her, upon this the poor creature crouched and shook all over, and, speaking in a timid tone, fell fast asleep. We were amazed, not because she was transported with frenzy, for that with her was an ordinary occurrence, but because she spoke in the Armenian tongue, though she had never up to that hour

---

dissipates enchantments, which is confirmed by Arnobius, Lactantius, Prudentius, Minutius Felix, and others. Lucian says that the oracles were chiefly afraid of the subtleties of the Epicureans, and the Christians.

[1] This, it must be admitted, is a compliment to the sex, as handsome as it is just, and, coming from a monk, is particularly gallant.

[2] This may be significant as Armenia was reputedly the source of the Thracian Euchitæ.

so much as seen an Armenian, and understood nothing but her connubial and domestic duties.[1] On her recovery I asked what she had undergone, and if she could recall to mind anything that had occurred; she said she saw a sort of darksome spectre, resembling a woman, with the hair dishevelled, springing upon her; that in her terror she had fallen on the bed, and from that time had no recollection of what has occurred. She spoke thus on her recovery. Ever since that event a sort of bond of ambiguity keeps me perplexed, as to how the dæmon which harassed this woman could seem feminine, for we may well question whether the distinction of sex prevails amongst the dæmons as amongst the creatures of earth; and,

---

[1] How is a fact of the nature here recorded to be accounted for but on præternatural principles? We do not mean to contend for the truth of the particular fact here recorded, but doubtless this, if a supposed case, was similar to other real cases that might have been adduced; else Psellus would not have introduced it in his Dialogue. Very pertinent to our present purpose is the following from Calmet's *Dictionary*:— "Some efforts that seem to be supernatural may be effects of heated imagination, of melancholy blood, of tricks and contrivance; but if a person suddenly should speak and understand languages he never learned, talk of sublime matters he never studied, discover things secret and unknown; should he lift up himself in the air without visible assistance, act and speak in a manner very different from his natural temper and condition, and all this without any inducement from interest, passion, or other natural motive; if all these circumstances, or the greater part of them, concur in the same possession, can there be any room to suspect that it is not real? There have, then, been possessions in which all those circumstances concurred; there have, therefore, been real ones, but especially those which the Gospel declare as such." (Calmet's *Dict[ionary]*. Art[icle]. Dæmon.) To much the same purpose is the following, from the *Encyclopaedia Britannica*:-"All that Revelation makes known, all that human reason can conjecture, concerning the existence of various orders of spiritual beings, good and bad, is perfectly consistent with, and even favourable to, the doctrine of dæmoniacal possession. It was generally believed throughout the ancient heathen world; it was equally well known to the Jews, and equally respected by them; it is mentioned in the New Testament in such language, and such narratives are related concerning it, that the Gospels cannot well be regarded in any other light than as pieces of imposture, and Jesus Christ must be considered a. a man who dishonestly took advantage of the weakness and ignorance of his contemporaries, if this doctrine be nothing but a vulgar error. It teaches nothing inconsistent with the general conduct of Providence; it is not the *caution of philosophy, but the pride of reason*, that suggests objections against this doctrine." (*Ency[lopaedia] Brit[annica]*, p. 58. edit[ion] Edin[burgh], 1823.)

in the next place, how could it employ the Armenian tongue? For we can hardly conceive that some dæmons speak in the Greek, some in the Chaldee, and others in the Persic [Persian] or Syriac [tongue]; and also why it should crouch at the charmer's threats, and fear a naked sword; for how can a dæmon, which can neither be struck nor slain, suffer from a sword?[1] These doubts perplex me exceedingly; upon these points I require persuasion, which I think you the most competent person to afford, as you are thoroughly acquainted with the sentiments of the ancients, and have acquired a great deal of historical knowledge.

THRACIAN. — I should wish, Timothy, to render reasons for the matters in question, but I am afraid we may seem a pair of triflers, you in searching for what no one has yet discovered, I in attempting to explain what I ought rather to pass over in silence, and especially as I know that things of this kind are made matters of misrepresentation by many; but since, according to [King] Antigonus, one ought to oblige his friend, not merely in what is very easily performed, but sometimes also where there is something of difficulty, I will even attempt to loose this bond of ambiguity [you complain of], reconsidering the matter which gave occasion to Marcus' discourses. He said that no species of dæmon was naturally either male or female, but that their animal passions were the same with those of the creatures with which they were united; for that the simple dæmonic bodies, which are very ductile and flexible, are accommodative to the nature of every form; for as one may observe the clouds exhibiting the appearance one while of men, at another of bears, at another of serpents, or some other animal, thus also it is with the bodies of dæmons; but when the clouds are disturbed by external blasts, diversified appearances are presented; thus also it is with the dæmons, whose persons are transformed according to their pleasure into whatever appearance they please, and are one moment

---

[1] The sword has long been an instrument used by magicians to threaten spirits or dæmons. Psellus even hints on a previous page at dæmons being sufficiently corporeal, under some circumstances, to fear being cut by a sword. There is also a tradition that spirits fear iron, and that may lend weight to the use of an iron sword in magic. -Ed.

contracted into a less bulk, the next stretched out into a greater length.

The same thing we see exemplified in lubricous animals in the bowels of the earth, owing to the softness and pliability of their nature, which are not merely altered in respect of size, but also in respect of appearance; and that in a variety of ways; the body of dæmons likewise is accommodative in both particulars: not only is it peculiarly yielding, and takes the impression of objects, but, because it is aerial, it is susceptible of all kinds of hues, as is the atmosphere; such is the body of dæmons, owing to the imaginative energy inherent in it, and which extends to it the appearance of colours; for, as when we are panic-struck, we first are pale, and afterwards blush, according as the mind is variously affected, owing to the soul extending such affections [emotions] to the body, we may well suppose it is just the same way with the dæmons, for they from within can send out to their bodies the semblance of colours; for which reason each, when metamorphosed into that appearance which is agreeable, extending over the surface of his body the appearance of colour, sometimes appears as a man, sometimes is metamorphosed as a woman, and, changing those forms, it retains neither constantly, for its appearance is not substantial, but resembles what occurs in the atmosphere, or water, in which you no sooner infuse a colour, or delineate a form, than straightway it dissolves and is dispelled.

We may perceive that the dæmons are liable to similar affections, for in them colour, and figure, and all appearance whatever is evanescent. In these things Marcus, as I conjecture, said what was probable; and from this time forward let not the question harass you, whether the distinction of sex exists in dæmons on account of the genital member appearing in them, for these, whether male or female, are not constant nor habitual; therefore consider that the dæmon which so much harassed the woman in confinement seemed like a woman, not because it was really and habitually feminine; but because, it presented the appearance of a woman.

TIMOTHY. — But how comes it Thracian, that it does not assume now one form, and now another, like the other dæmons, but is always seen in this form, for I have heard from many, that dæmons of the female form only are seen by women in confinement?

THRACIAN. — For this too, Marcus assigned a not improbable reason, he said that all dæmons have not the same power and inclination that in this particular there is a great diversity amongst them, for some are irrational, as amongst mortal compound animals, now as amongst them, man, being endowed with intellectual and rational powers is gifted with a more discursive imagination, one which extends to almost all sensible objects, both in heaven, and around, and on this earth. Horses, oxen, and animals of that sort, with a more confined sort of imagination, which extends but to some things, which exercise the imaginative faculty [as for instance,] their companions at pasture, their stall, or their owners; and gnats, with flies and worms, have this faculty exceedingly restricted, not knowing any of them the hole they leave, where they proceed, or whither they ought to go, but exercising the imagination for the single purpose of aliment[ation], in the same manner also the species of dæmons are greatly diversified; for amongst them, some as the Empyreal and Aërial are possessed of a very discursive imagination, one that extends to every imaginable object; very different from them are the Subterranean and Lucifugi; they do not assume a variety of forms, for they are incapable of numerous spectral appearances, not being possessed of pliability and versatility of person; the Aqueous and Terrene, occupying an intermediate position with respect to those already described, are incapable of changing their forms, but in whatever forms they delight, in these they constantly continue.

But you should not be at all perplexed, if the dæmon that harassed the woman in confinement appeared feminine, for being a lascivious dæmon, and delighting in impure moistures, changing its form, it naturally assumed that which is best adapted for a life of pleasure,[1] but with respect to the dæmon speaking in the Armenian tongue; that was a point Marcus did not clear up, it will be manifest, however, from the following considerations: —

---

[1] Spoken like a monk.

It is impossible to ascertain the peculiar tongue of each particular dæmon, whether [for instance,] such a dæmon speak in the Hebrew, or Greek, or Syriac, or other barbarous tongue; indeed, [I may ask,] what absolute need have they of a voice, who usually hold intercourse without one? [as I already observed,] but as in the case of the angels [1] of the nations, different angels being appointed over

---

[1] This is speaking very particularly on a subject respecting which we know little or nothing, "secret things belong unto God, but the things that are revealed," &c. We are not under any necessity for supposing, that angelic beings understand each [other], but a single language, they may have an intuitive perception of all languages, and hold intercourse with each other, in a manner, of which we cannot form the most remote conception, it is idle to speculate on such a subject. Most that can be safely affirmed respecting them, may be comprised within a few words — that they are innumerable — that they are God's executive — that they are vastly superior to us in might and intelligence — and are employed doing good offices to the pious. With respect to the manner and circumstances of their appearance, we cannot do better than cite what Calmet says on this subject:— "The discovery of angels has usually been *after* they had delivered their message, and always for the purpose of a sign, in confirmation of the faith of the party whom they had addressed; it is evident that the angel who appeared to Manoah, was taken by both Manoah and his wife for a prophet only, till after he had delivered his message, he took leave "wonderfully," to convince them of his extraordinary nature; thus the angel that wrestled with Jacob, at last put the hollow of his thigh out or joint, a token that he was no mere man. The angel that spoke to Zacharias, rendered him dumb — a token beyond the power of mere man, (e.g. an impostor speaking falsely in the name of God,) to produce: and so of others." Sometimes angels did not reveal themselves fully, they gave as it were, obscure and very indistinct, though powerful intimations of their presence. When angels were commissioned to appear to certain persons only, others who were in company with those persons had revelations, which indicated an extraordinary occurrence; although the appearance was not to them, yet they seemed to have felt the effects of it, as *Dan[iel]* x., 7 — "I, Daniel, alone saw the vision; the men that were with me saw not the vision; *but a great quaking fell upon them, so that they fled to hide themselves.*" Paul's vision was very similar in its effects, see *Acts* ix, 7, xxii, 9, and xxvi, 14, also that seen by the guards at the sepulchre, on the occasion of our Lord's Resurrection,

different nations, different angels must associate with each other, they use each the tongue of their respective nations; we may reasonably conclude, that it is the same way with the dæmons, for which reason some of them with the Greeks delivered oracles in Heroics, but others with the Chaldees were evoked in Chaldee, whilst among the Ægyptians they were induced to approach by means of Ægyptian incantations, in the same manner too, the dæmons amongst the Armenians, if they happen to go elsewhere, prefer to use their tongue [the Armenians'] as if it were the vulgar tongue.

TIMOTHY. — Be it so Thracian; but what suffering are they capable of, that they fear threats and a sword? What are they to be supposed capable of suffering from such, that they crouch with fear, and keep aloof?

THRACIAN. — You are not the only person Timothy, who has been perplexed on these points; before I heard your doubts on them I expressed mine to Marcus, and he to remove them observed, the various species of dæmons are bold, and cowardly in the extreme, but especially such as are allied to matter. The Aërial [dæmons] indeed possessing the largest share of intelligence, if one rebuke them, can distinguish the person rebuking, and no one harassed by them can be liberated, unless such a holy character as addicts himself to the worship of God, and relying on the Divine power, calls to his aid the terrible name of the Divine Λογος [Logos]. Those that are allied to matter, unquestionably fearing a dismissal to abysses and subterranean places, and the angels who are usually despatched

---

Matt[hew] xxviii. Angels being invisibly engaged in the care and service of mankind, we can have no difficulty in admitting that they have had orders on particular occasions to make themselves known as coelestial intelligences, they may often assume the human appearance for ought we can tell; but if they assume it completely, (as must be supposed, and as nothing forbids,) how can we generally be the wiser, does not the Apostolic exhortation, "Be not forgetful to entertain strangers, for thereby some have entertained angels unawares," countenance the idea that such an occurrence is not impossible even now.

against them, when one threatens them with these, [the angels,] and their being conveyed away to such places, and calls over them, the designation of the angels appointed to this office, [1] are afraid, and thrown into great perturbation; so that from being deranged, they cannot discern who it is that threatens.

TIMOTHY. — But what advantage, did he say, resulted from the service of the Aërial dæmons?

THRACIAN. — He did not say, my good friend, that any good resulted from those proceedings; indeed the things themselves proclaim in a barefaced manner that they are made up of vanity, imposture, and a groundless imagination, however fiery meteors, such as are usually called falling stars, descend from them on their worshippers, which the madmen have the hardihood to call visions of God, though they have no truth, nor certainty, nor stability about them, (for what [creature] of a luminous character, could belong to the darkened dæmons,) and though they are but ridiculous tricks of theirs,[2] [could] such things as are effected by optical illusions, or by

---

[1] Here the doctrine that demons can be constrained by invoking their corresponding angel is set out. The angels appointed to this office are listed in grimoires, where it is made clear that the invocation of the correct angel to control a specific demon is one of the methods used. See Skinner & Rankine, *The Goetia of Dr Rudd*, Golden Hoard, Singapore, 2007. -Ed.

[2] There seems [to be] here an imitation of what took place on the initiation of an individual, at the Eleusinian Mysteries; we are the more confirmed in this opinion, from this Monk Marcus being designated in a previous part of the work τελεστης εποπτης [*telestes epoptes*], an initiated inspector, the very technical phrase applied to one initiated in the greater mysteries — a year having elapsed after one had been initiated in the minor mysteries, (in which state he was called μυστης [*mustes*]); on the sacrifice of a sow to Ceres, he was admitted to the greater mysteries, the sacred rites of which, some few excepted, (to which none but the priests were conscious,) were frankly revealed to him; whence he was called εφορος [*ephoros*] or εποπτης [*epoptes*], i.e., Inspector [of the rites], ([Justin] Poll[ard], *Antiq[uites]*, vol. I, [page] 451.) Upon complying with certain rites, strange and amazing objects presented themselves; sometimes the places they were in seemed to shake around them; sometimes [they] appeared bright and resplendent with light, and radiant fire, and then again covered with blackness and horror, sometimes [accompanied by] thunder and lightning, sometimes frightful voices and bellowings, some-times terrible

[such] means [be] called miraculous? But really by imposing on the spectators; these things I wretched man discovered long since, and was meditating to abandon this religion, yet up to the present moment, I was kept fascinated, and my perdition had been inevitable, had not you extricated me [from my perilous situation] by the path of truth, shining forth like a Pharos,[1] placed to dispel the darkness of the sea, Marcus having spoke thus shed a flood of tears, and I consoling, him said, you can choose a fitter time for weeping, now it is seasonable to magnify your salvation, and return thanks to God, by whom both your body and soul are emancipated from perdition.

TIMOTHY. — Tell me this, for I long to know it, whether the bodies of dæmons are of such a nature, as to be capable of being struck?

THRACIAN. — Marcus said, that they could be struck, so as to be pained by a powerful blow afflicted on the person. But how, said I, can that be, as they are spirit, and not solid nor compound, for the faculty of sensation belongs to compound bodies? I am amazed, said he, you should be ignorant of the fact, that it is not the bone or nerve of any [which] is endowed with the faculty of sensation, but the spirit inherent in them, therefore, whether the nerve be pained or refreshed, or suffer any other affection, the pain proceeds from the immission of spirit into spirit, for a compound body is not capable of being pained by virtue of itself, but by virtue of its union with spirit, for when dissected or dead, it is incapable of suffering, because deprived of the spirit; also a dæmon being altogether spirit, and of a sensitive constitution in every part of it, sees and hears, and is capable of the sense of touch, without the intervention of organs of sense, it is pained after the manner of solid bodies, with this difference, however, that whereas when they are divided, they are with difficulty, or never made whole, this when divided, straightway unites, like the particles of air or water, when some solid body displaces them; but though the spirit unites swifter than speech, yet is it pained in the very moment of separation; this is the reason why

---

apparitions astounded the trembling spectators; their being present at such sights, was called αυτοψια, i.e. intuition.
[1] The ancient lighthouse of Alexandria built 285-247 BCE. –Ed.

it fears and dreads the points of iron instruments [1] — and exorcists, well aware of their aversion, when they do not wish the dæmons to approach a specific place, set darts and swords erect, and provide certain other things, either diverting them from that spot by their antipathies, or alluring them to another by their attachments. In these particulars, Marcus' explanation respecting the dæmons, in my judgment, seemed probable.

TIMOTHY. — But did he tell you this Thracian? Did he tell you whether the dæmons were gifted with foreknowledge?

THRACIAN. — Yes, but not a causal or intelligent, nor experimental foreknowledge, but merely conjectural, for which reason it most generally fails, so that they scarcely ever utter a particle of truth.

TIMOTHY. — Can't you describe to me, the nature of that foreknowledge, which is inherent in them?

THRACIAN. — I would describe it, if time permitted me, but now 'tis time to return home, for as you see, the air around is hazy, and charged with rain, and if we sit here in the open air, we will be wet through-and-through.

TIMOTHY. — Friend, consider what you do, leaving your discourse unfinished.

THRACIAN. — Don't be uneasy, my best friend, for please God, the first opportunity you and I meet again, I will make good whatever is wanting, and, that in the Syracusan style.[2]

---

[1] Iron rather than any other metal has this effect. —Ed.
[2] Literally beyond the *decimes* of the Syracusans.

NOTES.

Manes and the Euchitæ. — On the overthrow of the credit and authority of the Gnostic sect in the third century, Manes, or Manichæus, by birth a Persian, started up originally [as] a Magian philosopher.[1] He was instructed in all those arts esteemed in Persia and the neighbouring nations, and was thoroughly versed in astronomical science. "His genius," says Mosheim,[2] "was vigorous and sublime, but redundant and ungoverned, and he was presumptuous enough to attempt to blend the Magian philosophy with the Christian faith." Mosheim gives a long statement of his peculiar doctrines, which I differ in nothing from what is related of them in this work, except that it supplies many matters which are here omitted. It may astonish us how be could gain over partisans from the Christian body [church] to his fantastic system, the more especially as be prescribed the most rigorous self-denial, prohibiting to the higher order of his followers (the Elect, as he called them) not merely sensual indulgences, but the most innocent gratifications; he surmounted every difficulty, however, by announcing himself the promised Paraclete, who was to instruct and guide them into all truth.

By virtue of this his pretended character, he pronounced the Old Testament the work of the Prince of Darkness, and the four Gospels, he asserted, were corrupted and interpolated by designing and artful men, and embellished with Jewish fables and fictions; he therefore supplied their place by a gospel which, he said, was dictated to him by God himself, and which he distinguished by the

---

[1] Mani or Manes (210-276 C.E.) a native of Babylon, founded the Manichaean religion, a dualistic Iranian Gnostic religion which spread widely from the Roman Empire to China. –Ed.

[2] Johann Lorenz Mosheim (1693-1755) a German Lutheran church historian. –Ed.

title of Erteng.[1] He rejected the *Acts* of the Apostles, and, though he acknowledged the *Epistles* that are attributed to St. Paul to be the production of that divine Apostle, yet he looked upon them as considerably corrupted and falsified in a variety of passages. —

Euchitæ, or Massalian, (the former being the Greek, the latter the Hebrew, name), signifying 'praying-men', was a sort of general epithet for persons distinguished for gravity of manner, and was applied in the east with much the same latitude of signification as Beghard and Lollard were afterwards employed in the west, and Puritan in still more modern times; so that many truly pious characters, who dared to oppose the mummery and superstition of the dark ages, were loaded with the opprobrious epithet Euchitæ, in common with those who held most revolting sentiments, and who, from very different motives, opposed the existing orders of things.

Manichæans were also called by this designation. It was not till toward the close of the fourth century that the Euchitæ made their appearance as a distinct religious body, their name being derived from their habit of continual prayer; they were founded by certain monks of Mesopotamia; their doctrine, according to Mosheim, was as follows: —

"They imagined that the mind of every man was inhabited by an *evil dæmon*, whom it was impossible to expel by any other means than by constant prayer and singing of hymns." To this leading tenet they added other enormous opinions, evidently derived from the source whence the Manichæans derived their errors, viz. the tenets of the oriental philosophy.[2]

---

[1] The book referred to is the *Ardahang* or *Aržang* which was one of Mani's holy books, and contained many paintings. –Ed.
[2] The four other notes which appeared here in the first edition have in this edition been moved to the page to which they referred to facilitate ease of reading. –Ed.

Bibliography

Editions

Editions of Psellus's *On the Operation of Dæmons* are known in Greek (*Peri Energeias Daimonon Dialogos*) and Latin (*De Operatione Dæmonum Dialogus*) from 1576, 1615 (Drouart, Paris), 1641, 1677, 1688 (edited by Gilbertus Gaulminus Molinensis, Kiloni) and 1838 (edited by J. F. Boissonade, Nürnberg). This work was first translated from the Greek into English in Sydney, Australia, in 1843 by Marcus Collisson.

Printed Source Materials

Abano, Peter de, *Heptameron or Magical Elements*. See Agrippa *Fourth Book of Occult Philosophy*.

Abraham of Worms, *The Book of Abramelin*, Ibis, Lake Worth, 2006. [Edited by Georg Dehn, translated by Steven Guth]

Agrippa, H. C., *Three Books of Occult Philosophy*. Translated by James Freake [Dr John French]. Edited by Donald Tyson. Llewellyn, St Paul, 1993.

Agrippa, H. C., *Fourth Book of Occult Philosophy*.
First facsimile edition Askin Publishers, London, 1978. It includes:
Of Occult Philosophy, or Magical Ceremonies by Agrippa;
Heptameron or Magical Elements by Peter de Abano;
Isagoge: On the Nature of Such Spirits by Georg Villinganus;
Arbatel of Magick: *Of the Magick of the Ancients*;
Of Geomancy by Agrippa;
Of Astronomical Geomancy by Gerard Cremonensis.
New edition by Stephen Skinner, Nicolas-Hays, Berwick, 2005.

Betz, Hans Dieter, *The Greek Magical Papyri in Translation*, University of Chicago, Chicago, 1992.

Bidez, J., *Michel Psellus Epitre sur la Chrysopée. Catalogue des Manuscripts Alchemiques Grecs,* Volume VI, Brussels, 1928, pages 97-131.

Blumenthal, H. J. [ed.], *The Divine Iamblichus, Philosopher and Man of God,* Bristol Classical Press, Bristol, 1993.

Boeft, J. Den, *Calcidius on Demons,* Brill, Leiden. 1977.

Butler, Professor Elizabeth, *Ritual Magic.* Pennsylvania State University Press, 1998.

D'Este, Sorita & David Rankine, *Hekate Liminal Rites: A Study of the rituals, magic and symbols of the torch-bearing Triple Goddess of the Crossroads,* Avalonia, London, 2009.

Duffy, John, 'Reactions of Two Byzantine Intellectuals to the Theory and Practice of Magic: Michael Psellos and Michael Italikos' in *Byzantine Magic* edited by Henry Maguire, Dumbarton Oaks, Washington, 1995.

Empedocles, *The Poem of Empedocles.* Translated by Brad Inwood, University of Toronto Press, Toronto, 2001.

Fanger, Claire [ed], *Conjuring Spirits: Texts and Traditions of Medieval Ritual Magic.* Pennsylvania State University Press & Sutton Publishing, 1998.

Farone, Christoper & Obbink, Dirk [ed], *Magika Hiera: Ancient Greek Magic and Religion,* Oxford University Press, New York, 1991.

Gautier, P., 'Le De Dæmonibus du Pseudo-Psellos' in *Revue des Études Byzantines,* volume 38, 1980, pages 105-194.

Greenfield, Richard, *Traditions of Belief in Late Byzantine Demonology,* Hakkert, Amsterdam, 1988.

Iamblichus, *On the Egyptian, Chaldeaen and Assyrian Mysteries.* Thomas Taylor and Alexander Wilder translations edited by Steve Ronan, Chthonios, Hastings, 1989.

Karr, Don. *Sepher Raziel: Liber Salomonis,* Volume 6, Sourceworks of Ceremonial Magic, Golden Hoard Press, Singapore, 2010.

Kazhdan, Alexander, 'Holy and Unholy Miracle Workers' in *Byzantine Magic* edited by Henry Maguire, Dumbarton Oaks, Washington, 1995.

Lewy, Hans, *Chaldaean Oracles and Theurgy*, Paris, 1958.

Maguire, Henry (ed.), *Byzantine Magic*, Dumbarton Oaks, Washington, 1995.

Maternus, Julius Firmicus, *Matheseos*, trans by Jean Rhys Bram, Noyse Press, Park Ridge, 1975.

Meade, Phil, 'On the Dæmon' in *Theandros: An Online Journal of Orthodox Christian Theology and Philosophy*, Volume 1, number 3, Spring 2004.

Obolensky, Dimitri, *The Bogomils: A Study in Balkan Neo-Manichaeism*, OUP, Oxford, 2008.

Paulus Alexandrinus, *Introductory Matters*, Vol 1 of Project Hindsight, Greek Track, Golden Hind Press, 1993.

Peers, Glenn, *Subtle Bodies: Representing Angels in Byzantium*. University of California Press, Berkeley & London, 2001.

Peterson, Joseph, www.esotericarchives.com.

Proclus, *On Parmenides*. [trans John Dillon & Glenn Morrow], Princeton University Press, 1990.

Psellus, Michael Constantine, *De Operatione Dæmonum Dialogus*. Gilbertus Gaulminus Molinensis. Kiloni, 1688. [Greek and Latin]

Psellus, Michael Constantine, *Oratio in Archangelum Michaelem* in *Michaelis Pselli 'Orationes Hagiographicae'*, edited E. A. Fisher, Stuttgart & Leipzig, 1994.

Shaw, Gregory, *Theurgy and the Soul: Neoplatonism of Iamblichus of Chalcis*, Penn State University Press, 1995.

Shepherd, A R, 'Pagan Cults of Angels in Roman Asia Minor' in *Talanta*, 12/13, 1980-1, pages 77-101.

Skinner, Stephen, *Complete Magician's Tables*, Golden Hoard Press, London & Singapore, 2006; second edition Llewellyn, Woodbury, 2007.

Skinner, Stephen & Rankine, David, *The Practical Angel Magic of John Dee's Enochian Tables*, Volume 1, Sourceworks of Ceremonial Magic, Golden Hoard Press, London, 2004.

Skinner, Stephen & Rankine, David, *Keys to the Gateway of Magic*, Volume 2, Sourceworks of Ceremonial Magic, Golden Hoard Press, London, 2005.

Skinner, Stephen & Rankine, David, *The Goetia of Dr Rudd*, Volume 3, Sourceworks of Ceremonial Magic, Golden Hoard Press, London & Singapore, 2007.

Skinner, Stephen & Rankine, David, *The Veritable Key of Solomon*, Volume 4, Sourceworks of Ceremonial Magic, Golden Hoard Press, London & Singapore, 2008.

Skinner, Stephen & Rankine, David, *The Grimoire of St Cyprian: Clavis Inferni*, Volume 5 Sourceworks of Ceremonial Magic, Golden Hoard Press, Singapore, 2009.

Snipes, K, 'An Unedited Treatise of Michael Psellos on the Iconography of Angels and on the Religious Festivals Celebrated on Each Day of the Week' in *Gonimos: Neoplatonic and Byzantine Studies Presented to Leendert G. Westerlink at 75*, edited J. Duffy & J. Peradotto, Buffalo, 1988, pages 189-205.

Williams, A L, 'The Cult of the Angels at Colossae' in *Journal of Theological Studies*, 10, 1909, pages 413-438.

Woodhouse, C. M., *George Gemistos Plethon: The Last of the Hellenes*. Clarendon Press, Oxford, 1986.

Selected Classical References to Dæmons

Aristotle, *De Anima* 2.3:414b 19.

Empedocles, fragment 11/115.

Epictetus, *Dissertations*, I, 14-12 & 14-14.

Euripides, *Alcestis,* 1003.

Hesiod, *Works and Days*, 252.

Homer, *Iliad,* Book IX, 237-9.

Iamblichus, *On the Mysteries*, Book I, 6, Book IX.

Julius Firmicus Maternus, *Matheseos,* Libri IV & VIII.

Plato, *Phaedo* 107d; *Republic* 382d; *Laws* 713c; *Cratylus* 398b; *Phaedrus* 271; *Epinomis* 984e-985b; *Timaeus* 90a-c.

Plotinus, *Ennead* III, 4 & IV.

Plutarch, *Life of Socrates*, 588c; *The Obsolescence of Oracles,* fragment 23, *De Fac* 943a

Porphyry, *Sententiae* 32; *De Antro Nymphorum* X; *Letter to Anebo*; *Life of Plotinus.*

Proclus, *On Timeaus* 3.152, 165-7, 258; *On Republic* 271-2; *On Parmenides* 667, 829; *On Alcibiades* 31-2, 40, 68, 90.

Pythagoras, *Golden Verses*, 4, 36.

On the Operation of Dæmons

Index